MARIAN ANDERSON

(Annemarie Heinrich)

Marian Anderson

A Portrait

by

KOSTI VEHANEN

New York   WHITTLESEY HOUSE   *London*

MC GRAW-HILL BOOK COMPANY, INC.

MARIAN ANDERSON

Copyright, 1941, by the McGraw-Hill Book Company, Inc.

THIRD PRINTING

PUBLISHED BY WHITTLESEY HOUSE
A division of McGraw-Hill Book Company, Inc.

Printed in the United States of America

Written with the collaboration of
GEORGE J. BARNETT

CONTENTS

ILLUSTRATIONS

Marian Anderson

Song brings of itself a cheerfulness
that makes the heart to joy.

EURIPIDES.

THE EARLY AUTUMN DAY WAS FULL of life. The leaves were gay, in reds and yellows; the small lake shimmered in clear blue. A white-and-brown horse was grazing in the field; little chickens were busily pecking about in the green grass. The big black dog was walking by my side. Some planes from the near-by flying school were circling overhead, doing their daily exercises.

Not far away, in the hollow behind the big trees, I heard the pounding of hammers and the singing of saws. On coming near, I could see that the walls had steadily grown since the day before. The workmen were busy fitting one plank on top of the other.

Soon the roof would be shingled, and the occasional showers would no longer be able to interrupt the work. Then the electricians and painters would come to put the finishing touches on the small house, which already seemed to stand waiting for its mistress' arrival.

Even the little brook flowing near by appeared to bubble with contentment that the work would soon be finished. It seemed to know that a dream of many years was about to be fulfilled, years full of hard work and tiresome traveling. Marian Anderson's studio was about to become a reality.

Usually she came to see the result of each day's work after the last workman had left. This evening she came with flashlight in hand to inspect the small building that was to be the home of her art.

"Do you like this color? Don't you think the fireplace should have a marble mantelpiece?"

[4]

As I watched her going around, studying every detail, it became more and more clear to me that a cycle in Marian's life had ended and a new one was about to begin. An idea that I had cherished for a long time came to life. I said, "Perhaps now would be the opportune time to write our memories of the past ten years." We had often discussed putting down some sort of written record of our tours together. I thought it might make a book that would interest other people and give them an impression of the sort of person Marian Anderson is.

"Do you think we can remember enough for a book?" Marian asked.

The soft wind brought the fragrance of the ripe apples that burdened the near-by trees. Blue grapes hung from the vines that bordered our path. Just above an apple tree, the evening star was shining in all its splendor.

"Yes, I am sure we shall remember a great many things; but I'm afraid some will be forgotten."

"Do you remember Nina Grieg?" Marian interrupted. She was referring to Edvard Grieg's widow, the singer, who had entertained Marian at her home in Copenhagen.

"Of course I do! She gave you a little basket of flowers at the dinner table."

"Oh, I had quite forgotten that; but I do remember the lilacs Stanislavsky sent to me at the station in Moscow . . . and the champagne at Sibelius' home . . . and the charming Italian Crown Princess . . . and Mr. Toll, our very capable traveling manager in Russia. Where do you suppose he is now?"

"Yes, I wonder where he is, and so many others also. Will you help me to remember if I make the effort?"

"Surely I will," answered Miss Anderson in her low, soft voice. "Surely I will."

And to express my gratitude for her promise, I pressed her hand.

I had the feeling that this was the seal of the beautiful friendship that had existed between us during the last ten years and that will live always.

Later, before the crackling fireplace in the living room of Marian's new country home, we continued our reminiscences of the past.

"Tell me something, Marian, about your childhood."

"Why, Kosti, I hope you are not thinking of writing my biography."

"No, certainly not, but you can tell me a story of when you were a little girl, since I did not know you as a child."

"It is now such a long time ago that I hardly remember. A sunny day for me was a great joy, as my mother used to take me with her when she went for the milk, but on a rainy day she would leave me at home, and I had to miss the morning walk. So you see I always wanted the sun to shine. These walks continued until one day, when I was carrying the empty bottle, I fell. The bottle broke and cut my arm so badly that for weeks I had to carry it in a sling and couldn't use it at all. After that my mother would not let me carry the bottle.

"One morning my mother sat me in the next room in a little chair that had a sort of canopy top, saying, 'Darling, be a good girl. Sit here while I prepare breakfast.' I always liked especially to help my mother; so this morning I sat in the chair, screaming at the top of my voice. But I soon got tired of that, so I amused myself by looking up at the border of the wallpaper in the room. There I discovered things I had never noticed before.

"Wallpaper then always seemed to have a flowered border. Suddenly that morning the flowers all became people, real people, to me. I looked again, and I could see them begin to dance. Sometimes they kept in rhythm with my crying. One blue rose would change places with a purple lilac, and the blue forget-me-nots danced around a big chrysanthemum, and it didn't take long before the forget-me-not was a little girl and the chrysanthemum, a pink-cheeked cavalier; and they began to sing with me. Oh, it was beautiful; it was a dream. I could hear them all very clearly and see them too."

"It was a sort of prophecy," I remarked. "In the wallpaper the flowers seemed to turn into people; but in real life the people threw flowers along your path."

She smiled and did not reply.

"I also remember when I was about six years old I wanted a violin," she continued. "One day I was looking in a pawnshop window when I discovered a violin that I wished I could someday own. It was priced at $3.45. In those days I discovered I could earn five cents or ten cents by scrubbing doorsteps, of which there were many in Philadelphia. I saved my money for a long time, until finally I was able to go into the shop to buy the violin. I was sure it must be a Stradivarius. I remember asking the shopkeeper if it really was a good violin, and he assured me that it was. I was extremely happy the first time I held it in my hands and started at once to learn how to play it by myself. I played it for a long time—in fact, until the strings gave way; but by then it had served its purpose.

"I also learned to play the piano that we got some time after the violin.

"When I was in the grade school, I used to listen to the songs that were sung by the class in the room next to mine. I used to hum them to myself and always remembered them so that when I moved on into the other room the teacher was surprised to find that I already knew the songs that she had taught the class.

"I sang at church affairs when I was very young, and when I was only eight the neighboring churches, clubs, and societies would give concerts at which they would have me sing; and they billed me as 'the ten-year-old contralto.' My high school principal advised me to study singing and later introduced me to a professional vocal teacher."

"Is it really true," I asked, "that as a young girl you would often replace an absent singer in your church choir?"

"Yes, that is true. They used to sing an anthem called 'Inflammatus' that contained a high C, and I used to love to sing it when the soprano was away. I could also go to low D. My choir work is partly responsible for my sound musicianship."

"If you could do that when you were a young girl, what did you really have to learn?" I asked.

"Now you are asking a difficult question. I can say that I almost never practiced at home. When I came to my teacher, whether I had practiced or not, he would say, 'It is very good today. You were very industrious.' So I practiced only to learn the melodies of certain songs, for these were not already in my mind and voice."

"I am sure you had the qualities of a genius, even

as a girl," I said. "Can you say that some great artist was a real inspiration to you?"

"I can, definitely. It was Roland Hayes, whose singing I remember as the most beautiful and inspiring that I had ever heard."

We talked until late at night. The fire was almost out; only the ashes were gleaming. When I went to my silent room on the second floor, I looked out the window and saw once more the bright evening star, which now was surrounded by countless brothers and sisters. I sat down at the desk, took my pencil and paper, and began to write.

SCANDINAVIA

THE SEASON WAS OVER. I HAD JUST
finished a concert tour in the spring of 1931, and
was sitting comfortably in the beautiful home of
my manager, Mr. Helmer Enwall, in Stockholm,
discussing plans for the coming season.

He told me that he had heard about a Negro
singer who recently had given a recital in Berlin.
Some of the less important managers in Berlin had
written him about her. Mr. Enwall said, "I don't
believe those managers, or the critics; but a Negro
girl with the name Anderson certainly would be
successful in Sweden.* Don't you think it would

* The name Anderson is very common in Sweden. There are no
Negroes in that country.

be a good idea for you to go down to Berlin and hear her? I haven't the time just now."

"I shall be delighted to go," I answered. "I shall enjoy the drive, but I don't care about driving alone. Perhaps you could suggest someone to go with me?"

"I have Rulle in mind. I shall call him, as I know he, too, is eager to have new artists on his lists." Rulle is the nickname of our manager in Norway, whose real name is Dr. R. Rasmussan. He is well known as a playboy, is amusing and witty and popular with all the artists.

Rulle accepted the invitation, and soon we started out. We enjoyed driving through the lovely spring-like forests in Sweden. After ferrying to Germany, we were soon in Berlin. It was not difficult to learn of Miss Anderson's whereabouts. We were told that she was to sing for some managers in the royal palace in the German capital.

"That sounds wonderful," Rulle exclaimed. "She is going to sing in the empty royal palace." After the revolution in Germany, the Kaiser's royal palace was quite devoid of official activities and served only as a museum.

We discovered, also, that the Berlin recital had been Miss Anderson's only appearance in Europe up to this time. She had been studying in Berlin for some time. She was not at all well known in America, although she had appeared there a number of times. She had given recitals in Town Hall and Carnegie Hall; and had won first place in a competition among 300 contestants for an appearance with the Philharmonic Orchestra at the Lewisohn Stadium in New York. She had sung once with the Philadelphia Orchestra. But still she was faced with the difficulty of obtaining engagements. Finally, when she became convinced that it was quite impossible to build a career in the country in which she was born, she turned her face toward Europe, and not in vain.

Rulle and I walked down the lovely, broad Unter den Linden and over a little canal, on the other side of which was the old palace. At the side door we saw several people standing, waiting. They were evidently going in to hear Miss Anderson sing.

In the distance I could see a Negro woman standing apart from the others, who were busily engaged in conversation. Something in my heart told me, as I came nearer this young woman, that she was to be of great importance in my life. I couldn't take my eyes off her. As I caught a clearer view, I noticed

[17]

that she was fairly tall, slender, simply dressed in black, with a brown leather-trimmed hat. She held a bunch of music closely under her left arm.

"How do you do," she replied to my greeting, with a friendly, reserved smile. I spoke to her in German, since I knew scarcely a word of English. After a little conversation, we walked slowly into the palace.

As we opened the door, I was surprised not to see a large, beautiful hall. Instead, I realized that we were in the rear of the palace, with its old dark corridors. There were rooms on either side, arranged as if for a school, with benches and some small tables. We entered one of these rooms, where about fifty or sixty people had gathered. An upright piano stood in one corner.

Rulle and I went to the rear of the room and sat against the wall, waiting with interest to hear this young singer's voice.

Miss Anderson sang a short program, consisting entirely of Negro spirituals. At the time, I was unfamiliar with this type of music. Once before, I had accompanied a Negro baritone who sang them. I recalled that he had told me as we were rehearsing that spirituals were not jazz but the father of jazz.

This was my only acquaintance with these songs.

Before Miss Anderson rendered them, her accompanist told the audience the meaning of the words. The small audience listened in respectful silence, understanding that here was a singer who sang from the heart songs that she seemed to know very intimately. The impression I got was strange. These songs were quite remote from the kind of music I was accustomed to. The naïve words and syncopated rhythm aroused in me more curiosity than deep appreciation.

After the recital was over, the accompanist asked if we should like to hear Miss Anderson sing some operatic arias. We said that we thought that she had given us enough songs, thanked her, and departed.

Rulle and I walked silently for some time, each trying to fathom the art of this young singer. I finally broke the silence, saying to Rulle, "What do you think?"

"I think she is a marvelous pupil with a beautiful voice; but evidently she has much to learn."

"I don't know. I think the voice is well placed, without the guttural tone that most Negroes have."

"I don't mean the voice," Rulle replied. "I mean the expression, the interpretation."

"I think you are wrong. To me the songs sound like songs that she has heard from early childhood, and they probably must be sung in just this way."

"What do you think of her appearance?" Rulle asked.

"Sincere and charming," I quickly answered.

"Also on the big concert stage?"

"That is difficult to answer," I replied. "But doesn't even an unusual appearance have an added attraction for the average person? And with this wonderful voice, she really can become someone worth while. I can't forget the colors in her voice— not only one color but hundreds. If she succeeds in using all those colors to deepen the meaning of each word, she will be marvelous."

"But that is a long way off," Rulle said.

"Are you so sure? You know, Rulle, you may be surprised."

We both felt the need of refreshment and went into a restaurant, ordered coffee, and sat watching people come and go; but our thoughts were still on this unusual girl, so far from her native land.

After returning to Stockholm, we told Mr. En-wall our candid opinion of the young Anderson woman's voice and the possibilities we thought it offered. He smiled and said once more, "A Negro woman with the name Anderson must have success in Sweden," and immediately engaged her. This was the modest beginning of Miss Anderson's great career in Europe.

Mr. Helmer Enwall had a great influence on that career. He is the director of Scandinavia's largest concert management, *Konsertbolaget*. First, Miss Anderson was booked at a very small fee for six recitals in Scandinavian countries. As we know, this booking was almost as an experiment, because of her name. The question of the name Anderson disappeared after her first recital, however. Very soon her appearances were regarded as of greater importance than her name, and eventually there came a boundless faith in this young singer's future. The number of recitals soon grew to scores, then to hundreds. She completed three concert seasons in Scandinavia before she began her long European tour.

Soon Mr. Enwall was Miss Anderson's general manager and, as such, planned concerts for her all over Europe. It was not all smooth sailing; quite the contrary. At that time, most of the European managers were indifferent to Miss Anderson.

My first rehearsal with Miss Anderson was in my home in Helsinki, Finland. Here, for the first time, I heard her sing songs other than Negro spirituals. I began to play very softly, as though trying to get the pulse of the singer. Then she sang the first tone.

From where does this tone come? I thought. It was as though the room had begun to vibrate, as though the sound came from under the earth. I could not find the direction of the tone, but it seemed to me that the very atmosphere was charged with beauty—certainly the tone must come from under the earth. It made me think of an exquisite flower that stands alone in a deep forest, where no human being has ever trod, the roots drinking the aged nectar from the soil, rich with every substance that sun, rain, and fire can create. Such a flower blooms with a superb loveliness, with a most delicate perfume, trembling with a tenderness never before felt. So the sound I heard swelled to majestic power, the flower opened its petals to full brilliance; and I was enthralled by one of nature's rare wonders.

The voice not only has beauty but is soulful to the very depths.

Someone has said that if Miss Anderson were to sing the telephone book from the beginning to the end it would be touching and filled with deep, tragic feeling. Her voice seldom moves one to gaiety or joyousness. It can be likened, rather, to wide-open eyes filled with tears. It is also a voice of amazing range. At that first rehearsal she sang high C and low D, a span of three octaves, three times. It was real singing, without effort.

At first we had some difficulty in attaining truly artistic expression in songs. Marian's most important teacher in America, Giuseppe Boghetti, had placed much stress on expression and was not against taking unwritten liberties wherever they enhanced the projection of a song.

Considering everything, it is not strange that I often had an opinion different from Boghetti's or Miss Anderson's. My analysis of songs, though European, is also not always traditional. Marian often said that I had an uncanny way of digging out hidden meanings in selections, and this we played up according to a well-thought-out plan.

AT THE VERY BEGINNING OF OUR association, I suggested to Marian that she study Scandinavian music, which, at this time, except for a few Grieg songs, was completely unknown to her. She was pleased and interested in what I said, so we went to work at once. The first songs that I suggested were composed by the great Jean Sibelius; we also studied some folk songs in the Swedish language. This was the beginning of Marian Anderson's now large Scandinavian repertoire.

It was quite natural, when we went to Helsinki for the first time, to call Sibelius to ask if we might come to his home, where Marian would sing for him those of his songs on which I had coached her.

After speaking with him, I was very happy to tell Marian that we had been invited to visit Sibelius.

The awaited day came, and in the afternoon Marian and I drove out from Helsinki to Järvenpää, where the home of the great master is located. It is always a pleasure for me to visit him, and it was to be one of Marian's most exciting and profitable experiences.

Arriving at this wooden villa, of Finnish type, we entered through a small hall into the salon. The furniture is done in gold and white, Empire style, old and beautiful. On the walls hang exquisite paintings by the well-known Finnish artist, Gallén-Kallela. In a corner of the room is the Steinway piano, and on the piano stands a photograph of Queen Victoria of Sweden. The view from the two windows is very beautiful, looking out over forests and fields. In the distance we could see a large lake.

Next to the salon is the dining room, which is dominated by a large fireplace. Close to the wall is a long bench, in front of which the long Finnish dining table stands.

Next to the dining room is the library, which was the original children's playroom, now completely changed since the children have gradually gone out into the world. The walls in this room are of dark wood, painted nearly black. One wall is entirely covered with books, and the few pieces of modern furniture done in bright colors make it a most attractive room.

Marian and I arrived as it was growing dusk. In the salon all the candles were lighted in the chandeliers as for a festive occasion. Sibelius and his wife came toward us and greeted us warmly.

Mrs. Sibelius is a charming woman, with a beautiful face and rich gray hair. All her being denotes real culture and exquisite taste; her smile is very friendly, with a little suggestion of melancholy.

Sibelius himself is a very well-groomed gentleman. His handshake is powerful and gives one the feeling of great sincerity and confidence. Although it is known all over the world, his face must actually be seen for its power and strength to be understood. The expression of his eyes first impresses one; they seem to pierce everything with blue lightning; the look is cold and serious but quickly changes to a very kind and understanding one. Next one is attracted by his high forehead and deeply lined brow. His smile is bright, with an ironic shadow sometimes.

"Perhaps we shall have some coffee," were among his first words to Marian. I think coffee is not good before singing, so I suggested that we perform first, then enjoy our coffee.

I was nervous, wondering how the songs for which I, as the coach, was responsible would be received.

Miss Anderson sang two of Sibelius' songs, "Aus banger Brust" and "Sländan." It was not easy to sing for the great master in the small room, but since Marian was always calm and quite confident, she made only a little error in a few of the words. Her voice sounded superb in the candlelit room. When the last song was finished, Sibelius abruptly went over to the dining-room door and called to the maid, "Champagne." Everyone forgot about the coffee.

In making the first toast, Sibelius stood and expressed his enthusiasm with many kind words of praise, saying to Marian, "My ceiling is much too low for your voice." The only criticism he had to offer was the suggestion, "More Marian Anderson and less Sibelius."

We sat around the table, and I was surprised to see Marian drink champagne. She always has been very careful about using alcoholic drinks, but I think that in the delightful company of Sibelius she quite forgot.

The sparkling conversation touched many aspects of artistic creation and life. Mrs. Sibelius asked about Marian's mother and sisters, and Marian happily spoke of her family and told about her home. Sibelius, smoking his big, strong cigar, told many amusing episodes of his life in a way that only he can do.

The time went quickly; I saw the big cigar nearing its end. Marian and I glanced at each other. It was time to leave. After a hearty good-by, we went out the door that perhaps we shall never again have the privilege of entering together. Driving away in the dark, we both felt that this meeting with the great master had been far too short and that one of the most precious moments in our lives was now only a very pleasant memory.

Marian had the pleasure once more of meeting Sibelius briefly in the artists' room during the intermission of her recital in Helsinki, where Sibelius honored us with his presence.

In this recital, Marian sang a Finnish folk song as an extra number. It was a well-known song arranged by Palmgren, and she sang it in the original language. As I played the first few bars of the music, the audience, recognizing the song, sank back in their chairs. They were filled with eagerness and great expectation, waiting to hear how this singer from a race and a land so far away from Finland would render the song we all loved. The silence was so tense that Marian's knees began to shake, and only with great will power could she begin to sing. However, she rendered the song admirably; only in the last phrase her breath became short, and she took a breath in the middle of the sentence. The song had never been done this way before, but it happened that the pause came at just the right place; it gave to the meaning of the words a greater degree of beauty. I felt big tears rolling down my cheeks and could scarcely see the music.

The last tone vanished; no one moved; and after a stillness as of a closing prayer of gratitude, the applause broke out—applause so powerful that I am sure that we have never before or since heard such an expression of deep and sincere appreciation. Marian's sensational success in Finland was now assured.

As we left the hall, the people were waiting again

to greet her. It was impossible to get to our car. Only one policeman was on hand. He tried to clear a way for us, but he was utterly helpless. The people stormed around Marian in an effort to catch a last glimpse of her or to touch her dress. She was almost in danger of her life as we made a second attempt to get into the car. Her black lace gown was badly torn by people who wanted to have a souvenir. Finally, as we managed to get into the car, my foot was caught between the side of the car and the door. Just then a few strong men who were standing near by came to our rescue. But our chauffeur could not drive away until other policemen came. At last we were able to drive on, with the cries of joy ringing in our ears.

So Marian Anderson conquered a people who love her and will always hold her in esteem.

Before the subsequent recital I called the chief of police and asked for eight or ten men to protect Marian's life as well as her gown. He was most willing to cooperate and promised that we should have no more such trouble. And at every recital we gave thereafter in Finland we had sufficient protection.

Five more recitals followed. The sale of tickets broke all records. The box office opened at ten in the morning, but people stood in line from as early as the night before, and within an hour every seat was sold. I had many letters from poor working people who told me that after a day's hard labor they went and stood in line all night, and when they finally reached the box office there were no tickets to be had at any price. Many paid others to stand in line for them. People tried in every way, but, alas, the halls were not large enough to accommodate all who wanted to hear Marian Anderson.

The conductor of the Finnish National Opera was one of the persons disappointed. He telephoned me one day, saying, "Can't I come and turn the pages of the music for you, Kosti, as I would like to hear Marian Anderson, and there are no seats to be had?"

"Surely you may. I shall see that you have a seat at my side, but please do not touch the music."

In concert, I have never liked to have or to see a person turning pages of music, since it spoils the artistic picture. I have had some frightful experiences with people who turn pages. They turn them either too soon or too late; they turn them backward instead of forward; and often they turn two pages instead of one. But in this case it was very different, and I wanted to accommodate a man so prominent as the director of the Finnish Opera. The director was very happy to be able to come and promised faithfully not to touch the pages.

At the beginning of this recital, everything went well; the conductor friend sat comfortably beside me with folded arms, listening to the program with half-closed eyes. All of a sudden a page of the music fell down and flew behind me. I gave him a quick glance, thinking that he would understand the awkward situation; but he didn't move; he still sat enjoying the music and just stared at the fallen page, which was several feet away. I improvised the accompaniment for the song to the end.

In the intermission, Sibelius came to speak to the opera director. "What kind of musician are you? First you sit and don't turn any pages; then you let a page fly past you, but all you do is sit and dream."

"Why should I do anything more?" he said. "I was most emphatically forbidden to touch the pages." They both had a good laugh.

Eduard Hanslick wrote his name in music history because he could never understand or accept the great Richard Wagner; and his name is still an example to critics, warning them to be more careful about what they write and publish.

Some of Europe's sharpest criticism in the last thirty years was written by a man in Stockholm. His criticisms were widely read because they were brilliantly written, for all their sharp and ironic tone. Every artist was eager to know what this critic wrote about his performance; and he seldom wrote anything flattering.

About Sibelius, too, he wrote some very unfavorable pieces. It happened that Miss Anderson gave a recital in a little city near his home in a beautiful part of northern Sweden. After the recital, we had supper at the hotel, and the well-known critic was with us. In finishing our supper with some wonderful Swedish punch, I made the suggestion that we send greetings to Jean Sibelius, since two weeks before Marian and I had visited him in Finland. Marian seemed happy at this idea; but the critic said, "I don't believe Mr. Jean Sibelius would be pleased to have my greetings." I told him that I was sure Sibelius did not resent anyone's criticisms. He smiled and agreed to join us in the message.

Our waiter brought us paper and pen, and Marian began to write. Her writing is ordinarily round and clear like a schoolgirl's, but this pen was too sharp or something, and immediately a big blot appeared in the beginning of our letter. Another few lines and there came another blot; and a little later, a third. Marian was desperate. "We cannot send a letter with such blots to Mr. Sibelius."

I almost agreed with her; but our colleague said, "Yes, we will send this just as it is, and I shall take the blame for the ink blots." And so we all signed our names. In the corner of the letter the chastened critic wrote something like this: "I thank you for your genial music of the northern countries; what would they be without you? But you will see that I have made a great many blots in my life."

Here is another story about Sibelius. On a pleasant summer day, he was walking in a green-and-white birch forest in his native Finland. He was with a friend, and they were admiring the beauty of the forest, the mirrors of the silent lakes, listening to the songs of the small birds, praising the sunshine and the beauty of nature. Each bird sang

[35]

his own song of gladness. Suddenly a crow flew high and lodged in a branch of a birch tree. He was big and black, and in his simple way cried, "Cra, cra."

"That's the critic," exclaimed Sibelius.

Deep underneath the surface of this little phrase lies a great truth.

To quote more wise words from Sibelius: He was sitting at a table talking to a young composer. The composer highly praised the master's second symphony but added, "I still think that some measures in the second movement ought to be changed."

After a pause, the master, scowling at his critic, answered, "Do you also go to the Cunard Line in London and tell them how their liners shall cross the Atlantic?"

A third incident shows how mistaken critics can be. One morning I read in a large newspaper an article, evidently written by a critic, which said that Miss Anderson's pronunciation of the German language was so poor that no one could understand it. This made me a bit angry, and I was about ready to answer this critic when the telephone rang. It was Marian, who asked me to come down to the hotel lobby, where some newspapermen were waiting. I went right down and was introduced; and in one of the names I seemed to recognize the very person who had written that criticism of Marian's German. So I awaited the opportunity to give him my opinion of what he had written.

The reporters asked many questions, and finally this man asked Miss Anderson, "Why don't you sing the Sibelius songs in the original language? Why sing them in German?"

"What do you mean, German?" I interrupted.

"Yes, German," he answered.

"Oh, now I understand you and your criticism; those songs were sung in the original Swedish language, and I see that evidently you do not understand German," I said.

He blushed and without answering quickly disappeared.

When I visited Sibelius alone in 1939, he suggested many songs for Marian to use on her programs; and he gave me a song called "Solitude," which he dedicated to Marian Anderson. He told me that he knew all the Sibelius records and that Marian's recording of "Come Away Death" is the best recording of a Sibelius song in existence.

He was planning to move into Helsinki for the

winter, where he would occupy a new apartment. He was happy to learn that Marian and I would come again in the fall. And he invited us to come and have another pleasant time together. In leaving, he did not say good-by, just au revoir, and his last words were, "Do come again soon, and bring Marian with you."

By the fall, however, there were no recitals. Instead, the big guns and cannon thundered over Europe, and our happy dreams of again visiting Sibelius became a thing of the past. But his words, "My door shall always be unlatched for you," still ring in the ears of both Marian and me. When shall those days come again?

IN GOING FROM STOCKHOLM TO HEL-
sinki, Marian Anderson made her first trip in an
airplane. She had never been very eager to fly. She
is not really frightened, but she has a dislike for
the air, and experience has shown that she easily
gets airsick, just as seasickness affects her. She pre-
fers to travel in trains.

The sun was shining brightly, and light summer
clouds were in the skies when we left Stockholm.
One could scarcely find a more enjoyable and interesting route than the one over the Finnish archi-
pelago, with its millions of islands, some green and
rich with trees, others of shining red granite. The
forms of the islands are extremely varied and fan-

tastic. We thoroughly enjoyed the colors of the deep sea, the green of the verdant forests, the white of the waves breaking against the granite as though caressing the hard stone with soft, sudsy hands.

As we flew farther, the clouds grew more compact, and soon the beauty of the earth vanished from our sight. We were in the middle of the very heavens, far above the thick clouds and under the blue sky. The dark shadow of our plane could be clearly seen against the snow-white clouds, and around the little shadow was a glorious full-circling rainbow. This round bow of refracted and reflected light exhibiting the spectrum colors was a wonderful sight.

Marian was absorbing this unusual sight to the full and watching the little dark shadow that still followed our plane. Suddenly she broke the silence, saying to me, "Now I understand, if the good Lord doesn't like to behold the misery on the earth, He takes the clouds and covers it from His sight; but where human beings dwell there is always a dark shadow."

This remark, uttered quite soberly, is typical of Marian Anderson's deep and sincere, as well as simple, religious feeling.

I recall another trip Marian and I made between Stockholm and Helsinki. Every seat in the plane was occupied, but we could not see the islands, sea, or rainbow, for a very heavy fog covered everything.

The clocks told us that it was past time for our arrival in Helsinki. Through the door we could see the pilots nervously working, evidently trying to figure out the exact location of our plane. Finally I heard the motor slow down, and the plane began gradually to dip lower and lower.

The faces of most of the people were undisturbed, but those who had traveled by plane through the fog knew what a dangerous thing it was to try to land. Suddenly the passengers' faces were full of fear as we saw right in front of us the Helsinki radio masts. The pilot quickly turned the plane directly upward, and I felt as though my breath were shut off; many thought it meant sure death. I could not see Marian's face, but she told me that she had drawn her feet up on the seat in that terrible moment.

Unable to pick up speed again, the pilot was forced to fly down on the other side of the radio masts, and he narrowly escaped hitting them. This time we came so close to the trees that I could hear the rattle of the branches scraping against the wings as our plane brushed over their tops. The pilot shot the plane upward again. Finally, we could see the waves as we alighted on the water. We breathed easily once more when our feet touched the ground. The mayor of Helsinki happened to be on the same plane, and he came over to Miss Anderson to congratulate her and the others for getting safely through that terrible experience.

In Finland, we gave recitals not only in Helsinki but in smaller cities, some with only a few thousand people. Each time the concert hall was crowded. We appeared, among other places, in Viipuri, the city that was so badly ruined in the last Finnish war.

In Kuopio we took a sleigh and went up a high hill to a tower, from which we had an inspiring view. All the trees were covered with snow, and the branches bent down with masses of snow. To the north were clouds in marvelous dark blue and violet colors, hanging close to the earth; and in the south a brilliant sun was shining on the white snow, which appeared to be covered with tiny sparkling diamonds. The extraordinary sight made us feel that we were dwelling in a fairy-tale land.

In the heart of Finland we came to a town named Jyväskylä, where we gave a recital in the largest church. In the middle of our rehearsal in the church, we were surprised to hear people coming into the basement. Suddenly a high-ranking officer appeared in the organ balcony where we were working on our program. He whispered to me, saying, "You do not mind if we listen awhile? Finland's President Svinhufvud and his staff are downstairs. Please continue with the rehearsal."

Silently the President and his party sat in the church, and Miss Anderson sang as though no one were listening. When we finished, I closed the organ; Marian picked up her fur coat; and we were ready to leave. The President's adjutant came to us again and gave us the President's greetings, asking us to meet him downstairs in the church. We had to go through a foyer to get to the church auditorium where the President was waiting for us.

Miss Anderson felt somewhat shy, thinking that her rehearsal dress was not a very suitable one in which to meet the Finnish President. She would not enter the auditorium; nothing could persuade her; so I was obliged to explain the situation to the

President. He came into the foyer, and, after a word of greeting, told her many nice things about her singing. He then explained how he and his party had been on an inspection tour of the munitions plants located outside the city. As their cars came near the church, they were surprised to hear the beautiful tones ringing in the temple and, being curious, stopped and came in to find out who it was that was singing so wonderfully.

His last words to Marian were, "I assure you, Miss Anderson, this was the most magnificent performance that I have ever heard. To think of finding such rare beauty in this silent church buried deep in the winter's snow!"

For ourselves, Marian and I were sure that we had never previously rehearsed before such a prominent gathering.

In addition to the hundreds of concerts she gave in Scandinavia in 1930-1934, Miss Anderson spent two summers in the northern part of Europe, one in Finland, and the other at Mr. and Mrs. Enwall's home on a picturesque island off the Swedish coast, far from civilization. Here she enjoyed the life of a fisherwoman, sailing from one island to another, catching large fish, and eating them freshly cooked.

Another respite from her work later was spent in Sweden, again as the guest of the Enwalls. This was in winter. Marian often says that this was one of the most enjoyable Christmas holidays she has ever spent. On Christmas Eve everyone prepared to go to church, which meant traveling some distance. The snow was so deep that it was impossible to use the automobile, so the sleighs and horses were brought out and made ready. We all sat comfortably between big fur blankets, below which was a thick layer of hay. We wore warm fur caps that came down over our ears, and long woolen scarves. The most noticeable thing about us was our red noses. In a short while we were on our way, meeting several other sleigh parties headed for the same destination.

The little white church, with its high-gabled roof, was covered with snow. All its windows glittered with hundreds of candles burning brightly, sending out a welcome to everybody. We could hardly see the names on the tombstones that surrounded the little building, because of the snow and ice. Still we were able to wend our way along the little paths that had been made between the stones. People liked to come here to recall memories of other yuletides with the friends who had passed on.

Marian and I strolled around the silent place. We saw an open grave whose surface was covered with sand and snow. The walls of the excavation were lined with small green fir branches. It looked soft and inviting for those who were searching for ultimate peace. On the opposite side was a newly covered grave, overlaid with fresh flowers and leaves. The leaves seemed artificial in their deep green color, and the flowers, though frozen, still gave off an odor, as if greeting the cold wintry air.

It was like coming from the dead into a better world to enter the brightly lighted church, where, with grateful hearts, we were enveloped by the festive sounds of the organ.

After the joyous service, everybody started home. The bells rang out merrily to the accompaniment of the horses' hoofs on the hard snow. As the sleighs glided along, reflections from the lighted torches that each sleigh carried made fantastic figures on the snow-covered trees that lined our way. Forms from fairy tales danced along with us. We could see small figures of Santa Claus jumping around, big giants reaching out with their huge hands, a bear sleeping and, over his head, a cat, and, a little to the side, a slender white-veiled princess, waiting expectantly for her prince. From a distance this long procession must have looked like a glittering serpent winding its way through the forest.

On our arrival home, we all rushed eagerly to the fireplace, where the large yule logs were crackling. After warming up, we sat down to a delicious meal with a wine called *glög,* a very popular drink in Sweden during the Christmas season. This beverage put everyone in a festive mood.

Marian's eyes still sparkle when she recalls this very happy memory. It has been her sincere wish for everybody living to be as free and happy as she was that glorious Christmastide.

MARIAN ANDERSON IN SWEDEN.

JEAN SIBELIUS *(right)*, MRS. SIBELIUS, AND KOSTI VEHANEN IN
FINLAND.

ISS ANDERSON GAVE MANY BENefit recitals during the ten years of our association. An outstanding one, for the benefit of the Ethiopian Red Cross, was given in the Royal Opera House in Stockholm during the Italian-Ethiopian war and was attended by a very large and distinguished audience. Another important benefit was given in the Paris Opera House. Miss Anderson was promised the high French decoration, *Légion d'honneur,* at this time; but the little red band was never given her because of the disturbed political situation in which France was involved with Germany. In America she gave, among others, a large benefit recital for the Finnish war relief, the proceeds going through Mr. Herbert Hoover's committee. This took place in the Brooklyn Academy of Music in May, 1940. Miss Anderson has also appeared in hospitals.

A charity recital that I shall always remember she gave at a prison in Denmark. The prison is located in the outskirts of a small Danish city. We had been told about this place, where only criminals who had been sentenced to life terms were confined. Marian and I had some free days; so I proposed that we should go out and give a recital for those unfortunate men. We communicated with the warden of the prison, who graciously accepted the offer.

The next day we drove out. As we drew near, we could see the big, dark, dreary-looking buildings. We came to a large iron gate, which was heavily guarded, and drove into the grounds as the gates quickly opened and closed behind us. We were obliged to drive through another gate to get to the entrance that finally led to the warden's apartment. After greeting us kindly, he told us that arrangements for the recital had been made and that it would be given in the prison church. The church was too small to accommodate all the men at one time, so they would be divided into two groups, and the length of each program would be twenty minutes.

The first group was made up of men whose criminal records were not so grave as those of the prisoners in the second group. At the exact time designated, Marian and I were guided through many dark corridors and heavily guarded doors until we reached a small door that led into the church near the altar. At one side was the upright piano.

We were surprised to see that the audience was made up of nice-appearing, clean-looking men, who gazed at Miss Anderson with wide-open eyes, indicating their great curiosity.

Before the program started, the warden came forward to give a little introductory speech, in which he told the men that a great artist, Miss Marian Anderson, was very much pleased to come out and sing for them. His last words were that there should be no applause, since it would not be in keeping with the customs of the church in which the recital was being held.

Marian and I could hardly believe that these men who were so orderly and quiet had criminal records serious enough to send them to prison for life. But who can see into the heart?

Their faces seemed to change with every song they heard; at last there was a burst of laughter as Miss Anderson sang the funny little song "The Cuckoo" as her final number. This appealed to the men's sense of humor, and in their enthusiasm they applauded so strongly that it was impossible to quell them.

As the warden came forward and raised his hand, motioning them to stop, one of the prisoners spoke up loudly, saying, "We shall now sing for Miss Anderson." One of the guards put a song book on the piano for me, and so I accompanied them as they sang a well-known Danish song with great gusto. Marian and I were then escorted back to the warden's apartment while the groups of prisoners were being changed.

After a short time we were again guided back to the church, but in a different direction, through gloomy-looking corridors and heavy doors. This time we entered the edifice through another little door. We were now greeted by an entirely different group of men. The hard, cruel, and hateful-looking faces told us that these were the worst types of criminals. There was no kindly look of appreciation or gratitude to be found in their sinister, scowling eyes. On the balcony and in the aisles stood guards with revolvers in their hands, closely watching every move of the hard-boiled prisoners.

We couldn't tell by their appearance whether they were in any way affected by the songs; their facial muscles were completely motionless. No doubt any remnant of human expression had been lost a long time ago. But the charming little cuckoo song did its good work again. It was met with tremendous applause, but this time it was applause without smiles or any apparent expression of joy. It was almost hateful noise, though the prisoners seemed trying desperately to recover the last hidden bit of human feeling in their hardened hearts.

They also asked to sing for Miss Anderson. But the singing of this group was very different from that of the men in the first group. There was much more power and tenseness. My accompaniment was completely drowned out by these coarse sounds, which were like threatening waves in a stormy sea of contempt.

We then left, going down the middle aisle

between the pistol-pointing guards, and the heavy gates opened and closed quickly behind us.

A deep sigh escaped Miss Anderson's lips as she uttered quietly, "Lord, help their souls! help our souls!"

EUROPEAN AND SOUTH AMERICAN TOURS

IN THE COURSE OF OUR EUROPEAN tours, Miss Anderson gave recitals in Finland, Norway, Denmark, Sweden, Holland, Belgium, England, France, Spain, Italy, Switzerland, Czechoslovakia, Poland, Austria, Hungary, Latvia, Estonia, and Russia.

Of all the cities in which she sang, she found London the most difficult to conquer. The reason for this is not very easy to explain. She was always in good voice, and the programs were arranged to attract and please the English people. If I should venture an opinion, I would say the fault lay with the management and, perhaps, the English public, which, being conservative, is slow to believe even what it hears.

Miss Anderson's first recital in London was not well planned. It was given in a hall of rather small capacity, inadequate in every respect for an artist of her caliber, who was to become world-famous. Despite the fact that each time we made our three trips to London the sale of tickets increased, Queens Hall, where we later appeared, was never completely sold out.

In Switzerland we had a most agreeable time. Here we met Rudolph Holsti, the brilliant Finnish minister, well known to the American public for his work on behalf of the Finnish relief under Mr. Herbert Hoover in 1918. Miss Anderson's friendship with Mr. Holsti began after her first recital in Geneva. She sang in Finnish "The Little Finnish Folk Song," and did it so well that after the concert Mr. Holsti, with tears in his eyes, rushed to the artists' room to thank her. He was happy to hear his own language enunciated so well by a foreign artist.

He invited us to the legation that evening and said that he would also ask several prominent people who were present at Marian's recital. He said he was not sure whether there would be anything to eat, but he did know there would be enough champagne. He became a little embarrassed after our arrival, when he discovered there was no bread in the house with which to make sandwiches. Still this didn't discourage him. In his very charming way, he said, "That's nothing; that's a little thing that can be easily arranged." He himself went off in his car, made a tour of the different restaurants in Geneva, and returned laden with big baskets under his arm.

Many more times we were guests at Finnish legations. And here I should add that we were always cordially greeted by the Finnish ministers in the different countries that we visited. The legations were like home for both of us, and Marian made lasting friendships with some of the people whom she met there.

During our travels we were invited only twice to an American legation. This seeming lack of attention, however, was remitted when Marian was later invited to the White House to meet the President and Mrs. Roosevelt. Their hospitality and their deep understanding sounded a grateful note in Miss Anderson's heart.

Marian's recital in Geneva was given just at the time that the sanctions committee met there. As a consequence, there were many prominent men at Holsti's little supper party. The only person of prominence who was not invited was the Russian commissar, Litvinov. But when Mr. Holsti heard that we were to go to Russia, he made it his business to have Miss Anderson meet him.

The appointment was arranged for one o'clock on a day shortly afterward in Litvinov's hotel. We were there punctually, waiting for the Russian foreign secretary in the hotel lobby. He was late. The waiters at the hotel told us that he was to attend a large luncheon party there, in his honor, and that the guests, too, were waiting for him. After about forty minutes, we saw him arrive, a man of medium height, somewhat stout. He was in a hurry. He obviously had forgotten our engagement with him, because he was heading directly for the room where the party was being held. Mr. Holsti intercepted him at the entrance twice, reminding him of our appointment. Litvinov, seeing it was impossible to evade Holsti, stopped, bared his red head, and gave us a moist, loose handshake. He had a short conversation with us, and he said that whenever he returned to Russia he hoped that we should meet again in Moscow. We never did meet him again.

Mr. Holsti's insistence prompted Marian to voice an observation. She thought the most characteristic thing about the Finns was their determination to do a thing after they had decided upon it, and no one, not even the Russian foreign secretary, could shake that.

One night, while we were in Geneva, the Foreign Press Club and we were invited to a supper given by the city authorities. Many brilliant speeches were given in Marian's honor. I surreptitiously touched her foot and whispered to her that she should reply, and she did.

I have often wished that I could write shorthand, so that I could have taken down Marian's speeches at different functions; and I regret that they cannot be presented here. She is an excellent speaker and can speak at some length without preparation. The gist of one speech that I recall was her description of her inner feelings, as an American Negro, at being greeted in nearly all the countries of Europe naturally, without a trace of race prejudice.

We were quite familiar figures through many appearances in the Reformation Hall in Geneva, where, it is interesting to note, the first meeting of the League of Nations was held. An old lady, who had been engaged to take charge at the door of the artists' room during concerts, presumed intimate acquaintance with Marian and me. One time, during an intermission, several friends tried to gain entrance to Marian's room, but the obdurate old lady, exerting her authority, simply refused to admit them and went on to tell how well she knew both of us and that she adored Marian. Hoping to impress her listeners, she added a great many details about Marian that were products of her imagination. We heard about this later and had a good laugh.

We really enjoyed staying at the Beau Rivage, a splendid hotel in Geneva. In this same hotel once lived the beautiful Austrian empress Elizabeth, and here, too, she was murdered. The view from the hotel was enchanting. Floating gracefully on the blue lake were white-sailed boats, and in the distance ranged the snow-covered Alps, with Mont Blanc towering majestically among them. It was, indeed, a scene of rare beauty, of which one could never tire.

At this time the hotel was crowded with representatives of countries who were attending the sessions of the League of Nations. Anthony Eden was there, among others.

The Geneva Opera, like the Paris Opera and many others, was very eager to have Miss Anderson appear as a guest artist. Various opera houses throughout Europe have offered all the rehearsals that she felt necessary and explained that their doors would always be open to her. But Marian has always rejected even the most flattering operatic engagements. During our ten years together, however, I feel sure that she has not dismissed entirely the idea of singing in at least one opera.

She used to say that something within her prompted her to refuse, because the time was not ripe for her to step from the concert stage to an operatic performance. I suggest another reason for this. She dislikes working with people new to her, because she is hesitant about explaining to others how she wants to interpret a song and is reluctant to insist that a song shall be interpreted in her way. Often, in singing with orchestras, Miss Anderson has found that the conductor's idea of the interpretation differs considerably from hers. Because of the short time available for rehearsals, it has not always been easy for her to make clear to him her conception, and for this reason she has not always been satisfied with the results. The same situation might naturally crop up again and again in connection with any appearances in opera.

MISS ANDERSON AND MR. VEHANEN REHEARSING IN LONDON
FOR HER RECITAL THERE.

WE CROSSED MANY BORDERS IN Europe. On going into a new country, one is usually curious, and we were especially interested to enter the Soviet Union from Finland, though our feelings were somewhat different. Marian was seeing Russia, now the so-called Bolshevik heaven, for the first time. I had been fortunate enough to visit Leningrad and Moscow on concert tours during the palmy days of the czars. I was eager to see the change that had taken place in this huge, mysterious, half-Oriental country under the soviets. This last aspect, I may add, was interesting to both of us—to see a country that, to the outside world, is a big question mark.

The borderline between Finland and Russia was a small river, over which was thrown a narrow bridge with a single railroad track. The half of the bridge that belonged to Finland was painted white; the other half was painted red—the first sign of soviet Russia.

Our first stop on the border was at the custom-house. Here our train was held up for about half an hour because the authorities questioned us exhaustively about our phonograph and records. We told them that the recordings were of Marian's songs. They accordingly had a free recital while trying to convince themselves that what we said was true. Upsetting the train schedule made no difference to them. Apparently good music meant more than having a train leave on time.

We had further proof of the Russians' love for the less practical things of life. The Russian concert public is probably one of the most sensitive in the world, and it is a real joy to perform for these people. They show their appreciation by hand clapping, vocal outbursts, and stamping of feet; and one feels that their appreciation comes from the depths of their hearts. This enthusiasm was noticeable at the opera, in the theaters, and especially at the performance of a ballet. Russians respond quickly to things artistic. This quality is native to them. Even a new regime couldn't change this.

In Leningrad, Miss Anderson and I lived in the large hotel, the Europa. The furnishings were luxurious. Silk draperies were much in evidence, and large vases of French and German origin were everywhere. After a few days, several of the valuable, pretty vases and other things disappeared, probably to be used to adorn the suite of a new guest. The plumbing, alas, was in direct contrast to these lavish appointments. Bathroom facilities were seldom in working order.

Marian's first recital, like all those that followed, was sparkling, and it was entirely sold out. Before each group of songs, a woman explained to the audience the meaning of the words—a good idea in any country where the language of the song is not understood. We presented the same programs here as we had given in other countries, save that the management changed the titles and gave them a less religious tone if they were of a spiritual nature. For example, instead of saying "Ave Maria," by Schubert, they would say "an aria by Schubert." Exactly what the woman interpreter said to the audience from the stage when she translated a religious song is something for conjecture. We did not find out, but the changing of the titles made no difference whatever. At this first recital, as at almost all the others, the audience applauded for encores, and a favorite encore was "Ave Maria." To make known their wish, they just shouted "Ave Maria," and not "the aria by Schubert." What did this signify?

On going on the stage for her first appearance, Marian was surprised to find a microphone near her. Her contract for her Russian tour plainly stated that no recital was to be broadcast. After singing her first group of songs, Marian came to me and asked whether I had noticed the microphone and added that she hoped that it wasn't in working order. The woman interpreter, hearing what she said, wrinkled her brow and said in a decisive tone, "In Russia, one does not ask questions." We took this as a clear warning, and we both remembered it during our three tours in that country. We later heard that every recital had been broadcast.

Marian and I were paid in Russian money, which, of course, could not be used in other countries; so Miss Anderson was obliged to use it in the purchase of furs, jewels, and antiques. She was able to procure some very good pearls and diamonds, besides some lavish capes that had formerly been used in the churches. We discovered that Russian money could be used in second-rate stores but could not be used to buy commodities in the first-class stores. The latter wanted American dollars or European currency. We were really at a disadvantage in this respect, and I thought it a great pity that Marian had earned so much money but had so limited an opportunity of spending it.

The highest denomination was a thirty-ruble bill, and after many recitals, it became quite a problem to carry the money with us. We used to wrap the money in a newspaper or a bag, just as we would wrap a loaf of bread.

In Russia it is strictly forbidden to take photographs. I used to carry a small Kodak under my arm. One day, while walking, I saw a traffic policeman giving signals at one of the busy street intersections. His motions showed that he was a combination of actor and athlete. It was interesting to watch him. Discreet but intent, I snapped him, then calmly walked by. Shortly afterward, we discovered that we were being followed by the same policeman, who stopped us and pointed to my camera. Marian and I acted as though nothing were amiss, but I had clear visions of Siberia looming before me. I knew enough Russian to understand what he said to me: "Don't you know that it is forbidden to take photographs in this country?"

I answered, "Yes, I do know."

"Then why do you take them?" he replied forcefully.

"I shall explain. You are not the policeman who was directing traffic, are you?"

"Yes," said he, taking hold of my arm.

I replied, "I took the picture of you because you interested me. You looked as if you were acting and doing a pretty good job at that." My explanation must have flattered him, because he smiled and walked away.

One day Marian and I went to see the Isaac Cathedral, the biggest in Leningrad. It had now been changed to a museum. It was a keen disappointment to see this splendid church transformed. Among the things we saw was a mummy, bearing the inscription, "Can this body live after death?" Under the high cupola was a huge map, above which hung a metal ball that swung back and forth in accordance with the rotations of the earth. There were paintings of Russian homes before and after the revolution, comparing the prerevolution squalor and drunkenness with the comforts of the new age, comforts such as books, luxurious chairs, and, of course, the steaming samovar instead of vodka bottles. It all savored too strongly of propaganda. The Holy Room, behind the altar, had been changed to resemble a theater, and in it sat a toothless, witchlike old woman, shouting, "Here in this room, during the festival, we give the Mephistopheles scenes from 'Faust.'"

On departing, Marian took a deep breath of relief, and we both were comforted somewhat on seeing the big white snowflakes falling silently, as if to cover up the sins of the world. We never again went to an antireligious museum.

Among the attractions shown by the Bolsheviks was Tsarskoe-Selo, the former czar's palace.

We also saw the enormous and famous palace of Catherine the Great. It was filled with many gorgeous and luxurious things. A room that Marian especially admired was a large one whose walls were completely covered with meerschaum. It fairly shimmered with dark, golden, fantastic colors.

We were next guided to the late czar's apartments, which were in a separate house. They had been furnished in the bad taste of a parvenu millionaire. There were scores of photographs, littering every conceivable place. The most amazing room was the tiny sleeping room of the czar and czarina. There were two simple, narrow brass beds, over which was suspended a hanging lamp with two red lights. The lamp was a brass tube. Draperies hung everywhere. There were seemingly countless ikons, protectors of their majesties. Some of these ikons, given by Rasputin, the tragic monk, had merited a special place. They had been regarded as holy and more powerful than the others.

We enjoyed eating at the delicatessen in the hotel restaurant. We had caviar, of course, *blini*, vodka, and delicious chicken cutlets *à la Kiev*. We also tasted some of the wines from Krim. The wine called "Number 11" was excellent, and when we left Leningrad for Moscow I took a bottle with me. I thought perhaps we might need it during our trip.

Leaving for Moscow, we noticed the people on the station platform, loaded down with their belongings. To me, it appeared like old times. In spite of some inconvenience, we got to our destination in good time. It was an extremely cold morning in Moscow. The snow crackled and crunched under our feet. Men's beards and mustaches were white with frost.

Some people met us at the depot. I was surprised to find among them a face that was familiar. On first thought, I could not recall who this person was. Then I remembered that he was a former chum of mine who used to play tennis with me when he came to Finland to spend his summer vacations. He was part Russian and part Jewish, and his name was Kolischer. He was now an important man in Moscow music circles, the founder of the new Moscow Philharmonic. He was very glad to see me, as I was to see him; and our meeting brought back those happy, youthful days in Finland. It was through his influence that Marian and I were given preference, and we had two Lincoln cars at our disposal during our stay in Moscow.

During this, our first tour, we stayed at one of the smaller hotels. Here Miss Anderson did not have the comfort and attention that she had been accustomed to in the other European countries. The

[77]

rooms were furnished in somewhat the same fashion as the ones in the hotel in Leningrad, and the same thing occurred here. We missed the large, beautiful vases and the expensive draperies after a few days.

We visited only a few of the well-known show places. We failed to see the Kremlin palace, because it was closed to visitors. One day, however, our good friend Mr. Kolischer took us to Lenin's mausoleum. A word in the guard's ear admitted the three of us while many hundreds waited in line.

The mausoleum is imposing. The walls are made of highly polished stone. We went down a little stairway that led to the room where Lenin's body lay in a crystal coffin. The face and hands of the body resembled those of the wax figures one sees in the wax museums in various European cities. The head rested naturally on a red pillow; over the lower part of the body was thrown a piece of material that resembled a scarf. This also was red. The most interesting thing to me, on this visit, was the eager look on the faces of the people as they passed the body of the man who had been so important to them.

When Kaiser Wilhelm permitted Lenin to pass

through Germany in a sealed railroad car during the First World War, he hardly knew what power was contained in this little man and what an idol he was to become to the Russian people after his death.

Sitting in the large opera house in Moscow, one could easily conjure up the days of the old regime; but looking at the people quickly caused that memory to fade. We were forced to see that times had changed. At one performance that Marian and I attended, two little shadows brushed past, each with a bundle of newspapers under his arm, making for the front of the orchestra, where the boys used the papers to sit on. We could see these two little heads of disheveled hair as they enjoyed the music and occasionally whispered to each other. But this did not last for long, because an usher discovered them, came down, seized them by the shoulders, and told them to get out.

Tchaikovsky's works and all the well-known Russian operas were still in the repertoire. From the new creations, Miss Anderson heard some important music.

Shostakovitch's "Lady Macbeth of Mzensk" was the most significant opera we saw in Lenin-

[79]

grad. The last act, in which the prisoners are sent to Siberia, is one of the high lights of modern Russian musical drama.

During the intermission of one of Miss Anderson's recitals, we had the pleasure of meeting Mr. Shostakovitch. He had red cheeks, wore large rimmed glasses, and was quite young. He looked more like a student in agricultural school than the inspired composer that he is. We regretted that it was not possible to converse with him, since he knew only the Russian language.

In the theater, many new experiments were being made. These showed more or less good ideas but were still in the elementary stage. The famous Moscow Art Theater, under the leadership of Stanislavsky, gave the most finished performance, and it remains the most prominent in my memory. I do not recall the exact name of the production that Marian and I witnessed, but we still talk about the many scenes that were marvelously realistic and that showed the results of creative genius. It was difficult to compare them with anything that we had seen elsewhere.

Mr. Stanislavsky gave a tea for Miss Anderson, and, of course, I was invited. Upon our arrival at his apartment, we were ushered into his dimly lighted dining room, where tea was served in typical Russian fashion from the large samovar. At first we sat talking with his two sisters. Suddenly a side door opened, and the famous man entered.

I have not often seen such an aristocratic-looking gentleman. He was elderly, very tall, and his whole being showed great refinement. He had a clear voice, and his French was as good as a Parisian's. I knew that he was very much interested in Miss Anderson and her art, but I was surprised when he asked Marian if she would not like to stay in Moscow and study the role of Carmen under his direction. Miss Anderson may not have fully realized what an exceptional opportunity it would be for her to study "Carmen" with the master Stanislavsky. She smiled happily and answered, "It would be marvelous." But I wonder if deep in her heart she ever seriously thought of doing it.

Years later, when Marian was beginning to have a little more time to accept this unique proposal, she learned that Stanislavsky had died.

After the tea, we all went into his large studio, where several of his pupils and actors from his theaters had gathered at his request. Miss Anderson was asked to sing for this artistic audience, and she was most enthusiastically received. We did not have an opportunity to get well acquainted with any of the other artists. When we did happen to be in the company of anyone well known, it was always on a formal occasion and by invitation.

When Marian and I were about to leave Moscow, a greeting was received for Miss Anderson from Stanislavsky, in the form of a basket of white lilacs, which was placed in her sleeping car. It was amazing, of course, to receive flowers, so rare in the middle of winter, and we felt that only a great magician, such as Stanislavsky must have been, could contrive to produce them in the cold winter of Russia.

All over the Soviet Union, the batons of most of the orchestras were held by well-known European conductors. And all the larger orchestras were trying earnestly to be on a par with other European orchestras. We heard concerts conducted by Otto Klemperer, Oscar Fried, and other well-known leaders from Berlin and Vienna.

We also had the pleasure of meeting the old composer Ippolitov-Ivanov, who was very active in the Russian musical world. He was still privileged to live in his old-fashioned, comfortable apartment, as a gracious act of the communist government.

Miss Anderson and I were invited to be supper guests in this old patriarch's home one evening. It was a most pleasant evening, with friendly people who still observed the traditional manners. We sat around a large circular table, and the host himself served the food in a very unusual and amusing way. When he saw that someone's plate was empty, he would unfold his especially-made fork, which could be made to extend more than a yard. With this he would reach across the table, picking up the delicate meat pies before him, and serve his guests. The big samovar, steeping delicious tea, completed the picture.

Among the guests was the famous coloratura soprano, Nezhdanova, whose charm and personality appealed to Marian. This fine singer was very much interested in Miss Anderson's singing, and she came to every recital that Marian gave in Moscow, in the large hall of the Conservatory. On our first visit to Moscow, Miss Anderson gave four recitals, and on our second tour, nine recitals in this great hall. It was always overcrowded.

This hall was brilliantly lighted, and the only

bad feature was the old and much-used piano. Another thing to which we had to accommodate ourselves was the half-hour intermissions that were customary, to enable the listeners to eat a bite and to smoke and drink their beloved tea. Marian and I also were served tea and small cakes, which we enjoyed quietly in the artists' room. On the upper right-hand side of the stage was the government box, and in order to serve this box it was necessary to go through the artists' room. When the waiters passed through with trays of food on the way to the official box, we could see that the food was the same kind as ours.

At one of the recitals everything was quite different. When we went on the stage, the whole hall was in darkness. A strong beam from a large spotlight was thrown on Miss Anderson, and the audience could see nothing but the performing artists and the black piano. Miss Anderson, who is quite used to bright lighting effects, felt a little embarrassed as she stood in this very strong light; and my eyes were so blinded that it was very difficult to see the music in front of me.

After the first group of songs, I asked Mr. Kolischer, who always accompanied us to the recitals, why the light was so strong and if he would please have it changed. He told me, in a way that sounded as though he was frightened, that he did not know the reason and that he could do nothing about it.

When tea was brought to us during the intermission, we noticed three waiters, each with a large tray of delicious-looking fruits and baked goods, going through the artists' room into the box reserved for government officials. I asked Kolischer who was getting the exceptional service and special food. He again answered me in the same way, "I do not know."

After the concert, I asked others who the prominent people were in the important box, but no one seemed to know.

Miss Anderson and I still wonder who it could have been, and, although we never definitely knew, nevertheless, we always had our own opinion.

Before I proceed to tell of this trip, I must introduce you to two very good acquaintances who played important roles in our small family. They were Mr. Tolchinsky, whom, for short, we called Mr. Toll, and my turtle, whom we called Calle.

Mr. Toll had been assigned to Miss Anderson

by the Russian government to serve as administrator, or traveling manager. He was a small, friendly man who spoke a kind of German-Jewish dialect that one very often hears in New York. We understood each other fairly well. He admired both Marian and me a great deal. He would gaze fondly at my ties and shirts as if he recalled a time when he, too, had worn the same kind.

Mr. Toll saw to Miss Anderson's every wish. He would say smilingly, "Toll can do everything." Marian and I, in order to try him out, would often request the seemingly impossible. One time on a train, we asked for shrimps, and, lo and behold, the shrimps appeared. Another time, we asked for strawberries. He delivered these also. They were small and bitter, but nevertheless they were strawberries. Seeing a spot on Marian's dress or coat or on my trousers, he would take the clothes to his room and by some means or other would return them cleaned. Although we would discover the next day that the spots were perhaps three times their original size, we both appreciated his good will.

Mr. Toll, Mr. Savage, and Mr. Jofe were the best traveling managers we had during these many years.

To continue, I call your attention now to the

aforementioned little turtle, Calle. He traveled with us for a whole year, and he made his home in my coat pocket. His history is not at all complicated. I had often considered the desirability of having a small animal on our travels as a companion for Miss Anderson, who often sat alone in her hotel room. One day in Lyon, France, while we were having luncheon with Walter Rummel, the noted American pianist, and his charming Russian-born wife, a stranger with big sacks tied around his waist came along. He showed us the varied contents of the sacks, among which were turtles.

"Wouldn't you like to have a turtle?" I asked Miss Anderson.

"For goodness' sake, no!" she answered.

Mrs. Rummel was anxious to purchase one, and, seeing this opportunity to acquire an animal, I bought one for Mrs. Rummel and one for myself.

As time went on, Marian became interested in the turtle. She liked to watch his little red tongue as, in the trains, he sat on my knee, eating salad leaves. He became known on all the trains in Europe. We used to set him between our plates when we ate in the dining cars, and indeed he behaved very well. He was always served first. One night, because I was going to the theater alone, I asked Marian if she would allow me to leave Calle in her room. She was pleased to have him. On returning to Miss Anderson's room, I noticed that she was watching Calle from behind a screen. He was in the middle of the room, eating salad leaves. She quietly asked me not to disturb him.

Calle was not so well behaved at table when we were in Russia. One day, while we were eating caviar, some of the eggs fell on the napkin, and Calle proceeded to make some more crumbs on the napkin. Another time, when we were having dinner with Paul Robeson in Leningrad, Calle acted so badly that Miss Anderson told him to go under the table and stay there.

Although Marian is fond of animals, especially of dogs and cats, still she never becomes very familiar with them. When she is at home, she goes to the chicken house, opens the door very quietly and peers inside for some time before she enters. She approaches all animals in this way. She tries never to disturb them.

On this subject, another amusing story occurs to me. When we were in Paris, I purchased six tropical birds for Miss Anderson, which she greatly admired.

But the birds were early risers. They began to sing at six o'clock the next morning, preventing anyone from sleeping. Then they began to fight with each other. One red bird she named Kosti, because he was the ringleader. He became more belligerent as time went on; so Marian, saying that two Kostis were too much for her, gave all the birds to some of her friends. It was just as well. She had wondered how she would carry these very sensitive birds around with her during a cold European winter.

Mr. and Mrs. Enwall, of Stockholm, joined our little group, turtle and all, when we left Moscow for Kharkov in the Ukraine.

The important man in the Ukraine at this time was Postichov. He was called the Stalin of Ukraina. He gave especial attention to the cleanliness of the streets and thoroughfares. Large refuse cans had been placed on street corners because he wanted the streets kept immaculate, and apparently he had succeeded in his aim. The streets of Helsinki were the only ones I had seen that could compare with them for cleanliness.

In this connection, I should like to relate a little incident that occurred in Kharkov. On leaving my hotel for a walk one morning, I noticed a gentleman, who looked like an American, leaving the hotel at the same time. He was smoking a Russian cigarette with a holder. Eventually he carelessly threw the cigarette stub away. At once a policeman accosted him. He said, "Pick up that stub. Don't you see cans everywhere for refuse?" The young man made no attempt to pick it up. The policeman, becoming somewhat excited, forced him to do so.

"Don't you know our streets must be kept clean? Where are you from?" the policeman asked loudly.

"I am from America," the young man replied forcefully.

"From America; I see. Don't you know how to keep your streets clean over there? It would be better for you to go home and tell your people to throw cigarette stubs into refuse cans, where they belong."

From Kharkov, Marian and I took a side trip to Rostov. The railroad accommodations were extremely crude, and the journey took much too long. I suggested to Mr. Toll that we do the trip by plane. He seemed to be quite upset and repeated to himself, *"Flugi, flugi,* impossible to do. I am afraid something might happen to Miss Anderson."

We did not know the meaning of the word *flugi,*

[90]

but in Toll's language, it seemed to mean "airplane," just as when he would mean "elephant" he would say "folefant." We then found out that Toll had never before flown and that he was horribly afraid of a plane. But something told Marian that this was by far the better way to take this trip.

We entered a surprisingly small plane, which seated only six persons. Two of the chairs had been removed, in order to make room for several large packages. Marian and I were sitting in the rear seats. We could see that Mr. Toll was very nervous as he kept mumbling to himself, *"Flugi, flugi."* The only one who seemed really to enjoy the trip was little Calle, who was eating his salad on my knee and looking out the window.

After a few stops, when we were not far from our destination, dark clouds suddenly were seen in the southern skies, and in a few minutes we were in the midst of a storm. Our plane trembled and swayed from side to side like a leaf, causing the luggage to slide from one side to the other. The lightning flashed; the wind blew the rain against the windows, obscuring everything from view, and we were deafened by loud bursts of thunder. I caught a glimpse of Mr. Toll holding tightly to the arms of his chair.

The storm was of short duration, however, like most thunderstorms in southern Russia, and, on landing, Miss Anderson was warmly greeted by her admirers, who presented her with many bunches and baskets of varicolored flowers.

Traveling southward, we gave recitals in Kiev, the beautiful old Ukrainian capital. While we were there, we visited the famous monastery, Petcherskaya Lavre, with its lovely golden onion towers. This is one of the oldest monasteries in the world. From here we could look down into a valley and see a river flowing along serenely.

In the biggest church was a famous crucifix, about which a great many stories have been told. One of the stories tells how, in the year 1100, when the Tartars conquered Kiev, blood began to drop from the wounds on the Saviour's body, which hung on the crucifix. This seeming miracle recurred every time Kiev was in danger; and later, during solemn religious ceremonies, the blood would be given to the sick, blood that they believed could cure them of their diseases. Our communist guide told this story with a sarcastic smile and mentioned how ridiculous religion was and how difficult to explain. He said that the Bolsheviks had discovered a secret mechanism behind the crucifix that caused the "blood" to flow, blood that was made in Riga. He continued to smile sneeringly, although he never went to the trouble of showing us the device behind the crucifix.

We now journeyed from Kiev to Odessa, and we passed through a land of fertile fields and golden wheat. The weather was warmer, and our train seemed to be going through a cloud of dust. The dust inside the train was so thick that when I looked in the mirror the next morning I appeared nearly black.

Mr. Toll's face showed that he was tired, and we found that he had sat all night at the door of the compartment. He told us about a former trip with the well-known Spanish coloratura, Capsir, whose jewels were stolen from her during the night; so he warned Miss Anderson to be sure that all her valuables were in her possession.

During the trip, we frequently had tea, which the sleeping-car porter made in his own samovar. Once, when we asked the porter for tea, he came to us with a sorrowful expression on his face and said reluctantly, "Please excuse. It is quite impossible." We could not understand what he meant, but in a little while he came and told us that his samovar had been stolen in the darkness by someone who disappeared between the coaches. We did not know what we would do without our occasional cup of tea.

Mr. Toll looked more tired each day as he continued faithfully to watch Miss Anderson's luggage.

On the last day, Mr. and Mrs. Enwall, Marian, and I sat at the same table in the dining car. We were obliged to pick at the food, which was covered with a linen napkin to keep the dust out. Calle was the only one who ate his food without a cover, and he was satisfied with his green but dusty lettuce leaf. In order to keep my throat from becoming too dry and dusty, I drank some vodka. I tried to give a drop to Calle, but he was still busy eating.

Across the aisle from us we could hear some Russians talking, although they were scarcely visible. One of the young men came over to our table and watched the little turtle curiously. I asked him to sit down and have a glass of vodka, which he did. Suddenly we heard a young girl yelling, "What kind of a communist are you anyway, taking vodka from that foreigner? Don't you know how to act like a real communist?" The young man was frightened and tried to make an excuse, but nothing could possibly keep the girl quiet. Mr. Toll tried to calm her, and all the people in the dining car seemed to be disturbed by this commotion, but the girl continued even more furiously, as though she were giving a speech to a big crowd. Miss Anderson and Mrs. Enwall silently rose and returned to their car, but Mr. Enwall and I remained, for we were anxious to see how it all would end.

When the train stopped at the next station, the young man got off and soon returned with a bottle of vodka, which he gave to me in an endeavor to make good the mistake he had been accused of committing when he accepted a drink from me, a foreigner. As the girl went out, she coldly told the story to some Red soldiers. Soon one of the soldiers came toward me. Here Mr. Toll made an effort to explain the situation on my behalf, but the soldier sternly addressed me, saying, "Now is the time to go to bed, mister." And it didn't take me long to go. What eventually happened to the fanatic girl and the boy I never heard.

[95]

In Odessa, a very beautiful city, Miss Anderson's success was pronounced, and the crowds that attended the concert were most enthusiastic about her singing.

At the second recital, a boy begged me to take him in to hear Miss Anderson, since he could not afford to buy a ticket. I was very glad to do this, and I asked Mr. Toll to put a chair down close to the stage. The boy's face looked happy and pleased, but he never applauded after a song. This was not in keeping with the Russian custom, and it seemed a little strange to me. After the recital was ended, the boy came back and thanked Miss Anderson and me. We noticed that his bright eyes were filled with tears. I asked him why he did not join in the applause, and with a melancholy smile, he answered, "I could not, as I have only one hand."

Marian and I attended the Odessa Opera House, which is one of the outstanding opera houses in the world. Here we heard a mediocre performance of some Russian opera, but Mr. Toll was proud to have us see this great and beautiful place.

Often in the evening, Marian and I enjoyed a jazz orchestra that played in our hotel dining room. It was one of the best orchestras of its kind that we heard in Russia, and I am sure that it would have been appreciated, also, by a New York night-club audience.

One night, after supper and a few glasses of vodka, I proposed that we throw our champagne glasses in the mirror, saying that this was a Russian custom. The mirror was directly behind Marian's chair. "You don't dare," said Mrs. Enwall. "I think it is a good idea, but you don't dare," she repeated.

"I'll take you at your dare," I said and threw my glass against the mirror. The glass smashed into a thousand pieces. Many of them fell on the table, but luckily the mirror was not even cracked. Marian stood up, looking furious, and left the room. I assure you that I was ashamed and made up my mind that never again would such a thing occur in Marian's presence.

Mr. and Mrs. Enwall shortly departed for their home in Sweden. After a few days, we also left Odessa by steamer for Batum.

We boarded a large ship of modern design for the trip over the Black Sea. The boat did not leave on schedule, and we noticed that the docks were roped off and guarded, which looked to us as though someone was expected to arrive. The police were kept busy handling the immense crowds that had gathered at the wharf.

After a couple of hours, three elegant automobiles drove up. From the second one, a man, who seemed to be the one most honored, stepped out. He wore a cap that he raised as he smiled to the enthusiastic crowd. Mr. Toll told us that this man was Postichov, the dictator of the Ukraine.

The space on the steamer was divided into two parts. One was for the ordinary passengers; the other was closely guarded by detectives whose duty it was to protect Postichov.

Before arriving at Yalta, the famous place where the czar's summer palaces were situated, Mr. Toll came to Miss Anderson and told her happily that Mr. Postichov would like to hear her sing and that arrangements had been made for her to give a short recital in the salon of the steamer. He explained that it was quite impossible to refuse to grant the wishes of such an important man.

We were ushered into the largest salon, where Mr. Postichov and his official staff were waiting. His blond hair was standing straight up, his lips were thin and cruel-looking, his blue eyes seemed to bore through us. He appeared a sick man as he sat with his legs crossed, nervously shaking his foot.

I sat with my back to him as I played; so I could not see the expression on his face during the performance. After the program was finished, I noticed that Mr. Postichov had a tired smile on his face. Miss Anderson and I went to our cabins.

After Postichov left the steamer at Yalta, he sent Miss Anderson a telegram, thanking her for singing for him. This telegram was brought to her by Mr. Toll, who smiled triumphantly at Marian as he congratulated her on receiving such an honor from this powerful man. The curious thing about this was that Toll kept the telegram. Doubtless he thought that it would be wise to keep a telegram that had been sent by so prominent a man.

Our steamer stayed all afternoon in the harbor of Yalta. We had the opportunity to see more of this wonderfully located city, which was as beautiful as any city on the French Riviera. Mr. Toll, who knew about everything, brought us some splendid-tasting wine that had come from one of the czar's cellars. I had a table and chairs placed on the quiet deck, where Marian and I enjoyed the delicious wine. The sea was as calm as a mirror, and we could plainly see the reflection of the snow-capped mountains in the water. The place appeared to be dreaming of former happy days, this city of the once-powerful czars.

Gay dolphins played around our steamer, jumping high in the air, enjoying a last glimpse of the sun. Later in the evening we pulled away from this lovely, picturesque spot on the Black Sea.

All our travel on the Black Sea was most agreeable, and after the policemen and detectives left the ship, we fully enjoyed the voyage.

I lay all day on the top deck in the shadow of the lifeboats, feeling happy to be free from all the troubles of the political life of our times. Every evening the dolphins amused us with their playful pranks as the mild night fell quietly over the dark, calm sea.

As our steamer passed beautiful beaches and resorts, we drank in the grandeur of the snow-covered Caucasus Mountains that divide Europe from Asia. When at last we landed on Asian soil in Batum, we felt rested and once more ready for strenuous traveling.

From here Mr. Toll was obliged to return to Moscow, which made both Marian and me very sorry, for by now we were so used to traveling with Mr. Toll that it was difficult to think of journeying in Asia without him.

A new representative was supposed to guide us to Tiflis, but for some unknown reason he never showed up; so Marian and I were obliged to travel alone, which was not so easy, since the farther away from Europe we went the more difficulty we encountered with the languages.

We finally came to Tiflis and inquired when the first recital was to be given, but all the local manager said was, "Don't be too anxious; you shall know in time."

We had time enough to see much of this strange city, located in the far end of the Georgian Heerstrasse, the famous pass through which all people, for centuries, had to travel from Asia and India in order to get to Europe.

One of the interesting places in Tiflis was the sulphur bath where the attendants gave the massages with their feet instead of their hands, fairly dancing on one's body.

Here, too, we found the best gray caviar in the world, which must be eaten within three hours after it is taken from the water and which is much too tender to can.

On the streets we saw a great many mixed races. In this place, 125 languages (including dialects) are spoken.

After some days' *dolce far niente*, I discovered many large posters announcing that Marian Anderson's recital would take place the next day. Since we ourselves had not yet been notified of the date, I went quickly to tell Marian that her recital was advertised to take place the next day, which was surprising news to her, also. While we were talking, the local manager stopped in to ask how we were enjoying the city. A little angry, I said to him that at least he could have told us the date on which the recital was to be given. With laughter in his eyes, he said that the date on the posters that I had seen was a mistake.

"But how do you let the people know about the mistaken date?" I asked.

"When the people come tomorrow to the place announced, we shall say to them, 'Come back in two days.' This is the way we do here," he answered.

The recital really took place in two days, and the

large gardens were crowded with thousands of people, eager to hear Miss Anderson sing.

Another big success came when Marian gave a second recital, even without having a wrong date announced.

After this recital, we left Tiflis for the famous oil city of Baku, going by plane. Once more we had a nerve-racking experience when a bad storm broke and forced us to make an emergency landing. Marian and I sat on the bare ground of the desert for hours until our plane was able to fly again. We had to go through still another storm before we finally caught a glimpse of the Caspian Sea, with its rough waves dashing high. As our plane flew nearer Baku, we could see the extraordinary oil pools far below us. They were green and yellow in color and resembled some kind of poisonous liquid.

Our plane landed in deep mud, which was up to our knees as we struggled to reach the little waiting room where Marian, half sick and dead tired, sat on a plain wooden bench.

"Please try to drink some tea," I begged her; but she felt too tired. The place was swarming with flies. However, I boldly drank two glasses.

After being obliged to wait here for some time,

a poor-looking open automobile came to take us to our hotel in the city. The storm was still raging, and Marian's hat blew off near a slimy pool of oil as we were passing.

"I must have that hat. It is the only one I have with me," she cried.

I immediately jumped out and, after a chase, caught the hat, but not before it had blown into one of the oily pools.

We were weary and tired as we entered our hotel with the oil-soaked hat in our hands, but we were very happy to get out of the storm.

The artist's life is not always dancing on roses.

In Baku, the most exciting thing that happened to us was listening to a strange orchestra from the other side of the Caspian Sea. This orchestra gave concerts in the hall in which Miss Anderson was to appear.

It was composed of about sixty men, who played instruments totally unknown to us. At first they played calmly, sitting in their chairs, but when a moment of great agitation came, the whole orchestra stood up, held their instruments high in the air, and continued their exciting music.

To Marian and me the odd sight was more interesting than the music, which was only a rhythmic noise, utterly unenjoyable to European ears. The men's actions were impressive, however.

On the way back to the hotel, Marian remarked, "If these people here understand as little of our music as we do of theirs, then it is useless for me to give a recital for them."

"I think we shall try, anyway," I answered.

When Miss Anderson gave her program, she was greeted with storms of applause by the very same people who had so wildly enjoyed the strange music of that orchestra.

Happy are those people who can enjoy everything and whose ears are capable of absorbing so many different kinds of sounds.

Our next stop was to be in Kislovodsk, the well-known Russian summer resort, where, at one time, Russian millionaires came for cures. Here Marian and I were privileged to rest for a month as the guests of the Russian government.

We began our traveling from Tiflis over the Caucasus Mountains and through the Georgian Pass. We did not have a car, so were obliged to ride on a large truck with many other passengers.

The day we left, it began to rain, causing us discomfort in the open truck, but it soon cleared up as we reached the high mountains. The road wound upward in serpentine fashion; majestic forests bordered the way, and we had some wonderful views down into deep green valleys.

We stopped for lunch at a little house, where we were told that we could have the very best trout in the world. Of course, we were hungry, and the fish tasted excellent. Out in the yard that surrounded the little house, we saw a very interesting thing. There was a strong wooden pole, to which was securely tied a little Caucasian bear, which seemed to be guarding the place as faithfully as a watchdog. He resembled a large Teddy bear. We were told not to go too close to him, for he sometimes used his paws to molest the visitors. Marian offered him some cherries, which he carefully ate, picking the pits out and throwing them away. The little animal had a friend, evidently of long standing—a twelve-year-old boy who, we were told, was deaf and dumb. After the bear finished eating the cherries, the boy went over and, softly caressing the bear, sat down beside him, and soon their arms were around each other in fond embrace.

The road mounted higher and higher, the trees

began to be thinner and shorter, and finally there was none to be seen. There was more snow, but the roads were sandy and well kept. From the highest point, a marvelous scene unfolded before our eyes. I was surprised at the comparative ease with which we traveled; it was nothing compared with the big passes and dangerous roads in the Alps.

The Caucasus Mountains seemed to take on many gay colors, mostly red, green, and yellow, which indicated that in those mountains were many mineral substances.

As we went farther, we continued to enjoy it all. We made a brief stop where some children were playing; they were dirty, poor-looking, and quite small. They offered us some clear, fresh mineral water, which tasted most refreshing. One of the little girls begged Miss Anderson for a pencil. She fumbled through her handbag, finding a red-and-blue colored pencil, which she gave to the girl, who looked at it as though it were some big wonder and seemed to be as happy as she would on receiving a long-wished-for Christmas present.

After several hours, we saw some more children at a place on the road where we stopped. They did not offer us mineral water this time, but they gaily danced a wild Caucasian dance for us on the sandy road. Marian and I offered a five-ruble bill to the child who danced the best. The little winner waved the bill high in the air and shouted with joy. This caused the other children to become jealous, and a free-for-all fight occurred. Soon we saw the winner rolling in the gully beside the road, and I doubt if he ever found the money. As we drove away, they were still tumbling around and pulling each other's hair.

Marian kept looking back as she reflected, "Where there is money, there is fighting."

It was evening when we arrived at the city of Vladikavskas. We were still without an "administrator."

We found out that our plane was to leave very early the following morning. Marian was all ready at 5 A.M., but the hotel clerk informed us that the plane was not on time and that it would be much more comfortable for us to wait in the hotel rather than at the airdrome. The clerk would let us know when to leave, but the call never came, nor did the plane ever arrive.

There were no trains, and we knew that the roads were in a terrible condition after three days of rain.

We finally made arrangements for a private plane through the hotel management.

At the airdrome, we were obliged to wait another hour before this plane arrived. There were no other occupants except hundreds of flies. Marian, our guide, and I started the trip together, and as we soared higher and higher, a grand panorama passed before us: the Caucasus Mountains, with their golden-rose color of the morning sun on one side and, on the other, great stretches of cultivated land.

Our guide was a young man who liked to joke, and just as Marian and I were enjoying the inspiring view, he went to the pilot, asking him to do some stunts for Miss Anderson's amusement. Immediately the pilot began doing stairs and spirals. Suddenly we felt as though we were tumbling upside down, and Marian managed to scream, "No more! No more!"

I went to our guide to ask him please to stop these foolish maneuvers, since Miss Anderson did not like it a bit, but he asked the pilot to do it all over again. Then I grabbed our guide by the neck and forced him to sit down.

Marian felt relieved and safe as the plane

smoothly shot through the air. Soon we reached the Mineralnyvada airdrome.

Here we found it impossible to get a conveyance to transfer us to the city. After again waiting for some time, a horse-drawn wagon with a flat bottom and no springs came. We put our luggage in the center of the wagon, and Marian and I sat on either side, with our feet dangling down. The road was rocky, causing the rickety wagon to shake so terribly that when we got to the little station, four or five miles from the airdrome, we felt as though our insides were slightly mixed up.

In the evening, we at last arrived at Kislovodsk, where rooms were to have been reserved for us. Our guide, who had given us those exciting thrills in his plane, still accompanied us.

When we asked at the hotel about our rooms, the first clerk knew nothing of reservations. A second clerk knew all about it and smilingly sent for a bellboy to show us the way. After reaching the right floor, we were taken to the end of a very long hall, where the boy opened the door and, with a sweeping gesture that included the three of us, said, "If you please!" We, of course, told him that we could not possibly consider occupying the room.

It wasn't long before I found our local concert manager, and after talking with him I was happy to inform Marian that she was to have a room in a sanatorium.

During the three weeks we spent in Kislovodsk, we were able to rest. We took the baths and did some hiking, which gave us the needed limbering up.

Marian was asked to give a recital, which she gladly gave. In the middle of the recital, all the lights went out. There were only two candles to be found in the sanatorium. They were placed on either side of my music on the piano. Marian continued her program in the picturesque, semidark setting.

Although we could scarcely see the audience, we felt that they were enjoying the singing immensely under these unusual circumstances.

Marian took many baths in the Narzan mineral water, which seems to have curative values and which gave her renewed energy for continuing her concerts when we returned to Moscow.

On this visit to Moscow, Miss Anderson and I were invited to the home of one of the finest actors. His name was Yur'yev, and he was of the old school of acting. He had the good fortune to retain his old home, which we found to be so filled with antique furniture that it was difficult to move about comfortably.

Among his guests were the well-known theatrical producer Meyerhold and his wife. The evening was filled with gaiety, and the vodka flowed freely. It must be interesting to Marian, with her sober eyes, to see the effects of alcohol on other people, since she never indulges. Miss Anderson is one of the most tolerant of people, however, and never condemns anything or anybody—with perhaps one exception, the time that I threw the glass at a mirror in her presence.

Mrs. Meyerhold was no doubt a lovely woman, but her coiffure was so unbecoming and peculiar that no one could really see her face; the hair was combed far down over the eyes. Later in the evening, I could no longer hold back my open criticism of this coiffure, and rudely said to her, "My dear lady, your coiffure is really not becoming to you."

She showed a little feeling of displeasure and wrinkled up her mouth to answer, "My father said something to that effect, and he also told me that even a horse would be afraid of my hair; and it is really true. Horses are always frightened of me."

During our last days in Moscow, Marian and I felt fabulously rich, but we knew that all the money we had in our newspaper package would be good for only one day more. Marian did some shopping, after which I sat in a park. Here I saw many old, poor-looking people, sitting on the benches while the children played in the sand pile in the middle of the park. Some distance away, I could see an old crippled woman, going from bench to bench, evidently secretly begging. This is strictly forbidden in Russia.

As the woman came nearer, I could see her face, which was dirty and deeply lined. She had the look of a half-starved, aged woman. The gray hair hung in strings under an old shabby hat, and she had a very helpless expression in her eyes. As she hobbled over toward me, I took my largest bill from my pocket, folded it, and hid it in my closed hand.

When she was in front of me, I slipped the bill in her palm. She was not able to hide her curiosity and, unfolding it, saw that it was of a large denomination. The tears began to roll down her face as she cried with joy. She threw away her crutches

[113]

and fell down at my feet and began to kiss my dusty shoes. She held my foot so tightly that I could feel her trembling, and it was difficult to free it from her grasp. This was a touching and heartbreaking sight.

People began to notice what was going on. Children gathered around, and in the distance I could see a policeman coming in our direction. I again spoke to her, saying, "Please don't do that. Please let go of my foot. The police are coming this way."

She folded the bill with unbelievable speed, caught hold of her crutches, and disappeared in the bushes like a ghost.

As we arrived at the railroad station later on, many people were there to see Marian and me off. There were Mr. Toll, with tears in his eyes, Mr. Kolischer, and some other friends.

In saying good-by to her friends, Marian took her handkerchief from her handbag. In doing this, she dropped many little things, such as keys, lipstick, vanity case, and, above all, some loose diamonds, which rolled around on the station platform.

Mr. Toll screamed, "Marian, Marian, your diamonds!"

She laughingly asked him to pick them up, as she continued with her handshaking. This was the last time that Mr. Toll had the opportunity of looking after Miss Anderson's welfare.

Slowly the train began to move, and soon holy Russia, this big country of strange contradictions, was only a memory.

Good-by, Russia, with its crutches and diamonds.

MISS ANDERSON GAVE THREE RE-
citals in the Salle Gaveau in Paris in the spring of
1934. These were suggested by the ingenious Mr.
Helmer Enwall, her general manager, who arranged
for all her appearances in Europe. They were most
successful and were really the beginning of her
world-wide reputation.

It is interesting to note that the first recital was
greeted by only a small audience; but the second
was entirely sold out. I had read only one criticism between the two recitals; so one can see that
the music lovers of Paris do not rush to read a critic's
views as a guide.

The public in most countries of the world follows

the critics, but the French form their own opinions. If they like an artist, they will fill the halls; if they do not like him, the halls are empty. One reason for this may be that in Paris the criticism usually appears in the newspapers some time after the concert takes place, sometimes a week, occasionally several weeks. So if an artist gives two recitals close together, the public has had no criticism to guide it.

After the Salle Gaveau concerts, Miss Anderson received almost too many offers for engagements. Managers came by plane from Italy, Spain, Belgium, and each of them eagerly opened the door to concerts in his country, doors that until then had seemingly been closed to her. There were enough appearances possible now to assure the managers that they would receive large percentages, although in the very beginning there had been some deficits. It took but a short time before important managers from still other countries began to realize what they had been missing. Soon they began to get busy, too.

Among these managers, I remember with pleasure the Paris manager, Mr. Fritz Horwitz. It was he who made arrangements through her American manager, Mr. S. Hurok, for Miss Anderson's appearances in North and South America and in Australia.

Of the many local managers we have met in different countries, I am sure Miss Anderson has lasting memories. Certain important differences with them were avoided through her good common sense and desire to conduct everything in a calm and straightforward way.

The first recital Miss Anderson gave in Rome was held in Santa Cecilia Hall, a place filled with rich tradition, which inspired in us a feeling of great respect. The hall was so crowded that many people had to be seated on the stage.

It is always difficult to have an audience both in front of and behind an artist. But Miss Anderson occasionally turned and faced the group on the stage.

(In another recital at which the stage was filled, I remember, a deaf woman sat beside the piano close to me. She was trying to enjoy the singing through her long horn but was evidently unable to hear anything when Miss Anderson sang facing the large audience. The woman was desperate and asked me please to have Miss Anderson sing just one song facing the stage audience, of which she was a part. I nodded my head in approval, but the lady had not enough patience to wait. So after a group of songs, she left the stage and went down into the orchestra, where she stood up in front of the place where Miss Anderson would stand and put her horn high up, ready to listen. In the artists' room I had just asked Marian to face the stage audience when we went back to continue the program. This she did—of course, with her back to the main audience. I happened to see the deaf lady standing in the orchestra and the disappointed look in her eyes. After the song, the woman again rushed to her place on the stage. But this time Marian turned the other way to sing. Miss Anderson never saw the woman; and the woman never heard Marian sing.)

It was now four o'clock. We were awaiting the signal to begin the recital, and we could see that the audience was full of expectation, sitting with their faces turned toward the balcony where the royal box was situated and wondering who was to occupy it on this occasion.

Finally the Crown Princess Marie José and her suite entered and took their places in the box.

It is exciting to give a recital to an Italian audience; there is no crowd in the world to equal them. They applaud wildly when they like the songs, but numbers they don't care for they meet with a dead silence, no matter how great the artist may be. With other audiences there is more or less a set convention regarding applause, whether they especially like the numbers or not. Perhaps they feel obliged to be kind or polite to the artist. But the Italians are very different. Any artist appearing in Italy must get used to this unusual reaction.

Miss Anderson had given some recitals in northern Italy, where we had some odd experiences. In one recital, the applause was unusually strong except after one number, which the people received almost in silence. On coming to the artists' room during this silence, we both felt rather uncomfortable. But by the time we reached Rome we were used to such things, and nothing could possibly disturb Miss Anderson's calm fortitude.

During the intermission of the recital, Count San Martino came back to see us, and, on behalf of the Crown Princess, requested Marian and me to appear at the royal box after the program was concluded. We had previously known that the Princess was very fond of music and was an accomplished pianist. Immediately after the last number, we were ushered from the artists' room into the royal box.

The Crown Princess is a charming, tall, stately woman, and she greeted us cordially. She had a cold and regal air but paid Marian some very lovely compliments. After a short conversation, the Princess invited us to come to her home at the Quirinal Palace on the following day at five o'clock. Count San Martino asked me to bring some music and said that he would be our escort. He is the head of the Saint Cecilia Academy and is, of course, prominent in court and music circles.

Arriving at the royal palace at five minutes to five, we were ushered into a large room where all the guests were assembling. All the men on the Princess' personal staff, I noticed, including the elevator operator, were over six feet tall. They were dressed in brilliant uniforms and were kept busy with their pompous saluting. The lady-in-waiting greeted us sweetly but formally and introduced us to about thirty-five other guests, among whom were four queens and many princesses and princes—too many to count.

The last person to enter was a young prince whose shoes were very squeaky but who did not seem to be at all disturbed. This seemed to amuse Marian, and she whispered to me, "Poor prince."

At last the big door swung open, and we all entered a gorgeous room that was the music salon of the Crown Princess. She stood in the center of the room, exquisitely gowned in dark blue, with a bracelet of large pearls, the most beautiful I have ever seen. She gracefully and formally assigned me to the piano. Miss Anderson came forward, and we gave a short program.

After singing five songs, we were shown into the next room, where all the guests participated in tea and refreshments. The little child of the Crown Princess was carried in by her proud nurse; she was a lovely baby with bright, dark eyes, and though such a little girl, held her head high in true royal fashion. Only the queens were allowed to be near and caress the baby. Marian and I stood a little farther away.

After partaking of the refreshments, we returned to the salon, where we continued the program. An aristocratic gentleman of high Italian rank asked Miss Anderson if she would kindly sing a song that he had especially liked at the recital of the previous day. At first Marian was uncertain just what to do, since the Crown Princess was the hostess and had chosen the songs to be sung. But the gentleman fairly insisted, so Miss Anderson granted his wish and sang the song.

At the end of the recital, the Crown Princess asked for an extra number, which was, of course, given. After the closing song, Marian and I were not sure whether we were expected to remain or if we were free to leave. We made a little effort to move, but Count San Martino, seeing our intentions, came over and, touching Miss Anderson on the arm, whispered softly, "Please, please, first the *queens.*" So everyone left the room according to his rank, and we were the last to go.

The Crown Princess thanked Miss Anderson and said to me, "You must promise to write and let me know when you shall both come to Italy again, for I should like to have you give a large recital at my home in Napoli."

As we drove away from the beautiful palace, the count asked us what we should like to have as a remembrance from the Crown Princess. He probably meant some kind of decoration, but Miss Anderson told him that we should both like to have a photograph of the Crown Princess.

A few weeks later, when we were in Paris, a special courier from the Italian legation came to our hotel and presented us with magnificent autographed photographs in tasteful, artistic frames. It was an especially grand gift, which Marian deeply appreciated.

Very often during our travels, I saw this photograph on Marian's desk in her hotel room. I am sure that when Miss Anderson looked at this picture of the lovely Crown Princess, she was often dreaming of another recital in our charming hostess' palace.

UNTIL RECENTLY, SALZBURG'S NAME had much the same glory in the world of music as Bayreuth's had about fifty years ago. In summer, each place was crowded with visitors, who came to quench their thirst for excellent music. However, in Bayreuth, everything was centered around the name of one great composer, whereas in Salzburg, the attraction was in the names of the best conductors. The outstanding and most brilliant of these was Arturo Toscanini.

It was natural for well-known artists to gather where they could be closely associated with famous conductors. Finally, the whole musical world held their summer meetings and music festivals in the beautiful city of Salzburg. The lovely old town is an ideal place for the purpose, and the name of Mozart seems to hold a hand of blessing over the music performed there.

Marian Anderson's recital was given in the Mozarteum in the summer of 1935, but she was not then well enough known to attract the crowds. In Salzburg, this young artist as yet was only a rumor. Many invitations were sent out for her recital, among them one to Arturo Toscanini. But few persons attended; the hall was not nearly filled. However, enough prominent people were there for the news of Marian Anderson's artistry to spread around; soon her name was on everybody's lips. She had quietly gained the attention and the confidence of the influential musicians.

At this time, Mrs. Gertrude Moulton, an American woman of note, was staying in Salzburg. She was a great lover of music and was especially interested that her native land should be represented through Marian Anderson's art. She was positive that in this place, where the most famous figures in the musical world were gathered, Marian Anderson's name belonged among those at the top. She accordingly arranged a private recital for Miss Anderson and invited all the celebrities whom she knew in Salzburg. Since she did not have the pleasure of Mr. Toscanini's acquaintance, his name was not included. Rumors about Marian and her great art had already reached the ears of Toscanini, however. He expressed his desire to attend, and the invitation was, of course, sent. This interest that Toscanini showed made Marian feel very happy.

Seldom have I seen an audience like the one that came to hear Miss Anderson. It was made up of all the people most famous in the art world who were then in Salzburg. In the first row, in the midst of other religious personages, sat the cardinal archbishop of the town. His decorative robe and priestly hat were in striking contrast to the others' monotone afternoon dress.

All the conductors and many singers, beginning with Lotte Lehmann, were also present.

Miss Anderson gave a short program, including some Schubert songs, Brahms's "Die Mainacht," and some Negro spirituals, among which was one of her best, entitled "Crucifixion."

After the last song, Toscanini and Bruno Walter came backstage and thanked Marian. During the tea that was later served, everyone surrounded her

[129]

as she sat at the cardinal's table. They were all most eager to express their admiration; only one well-known singer sailed out of the room without a word of greeting to Marian.

I could repeat here many flattering words that were spoken about the art of Marian Anderson at this time, but I shall tell of only one instance, which, I am sure, is the most important. Arturo Toscanini told Mme. Cahier, "What I heard today one is privileged to hear only once in a hundred years." He did not say the voice he heard, but *what* he heard—not the voice alone but the whole art. And as I write this, I know that the entire music world is in accord with what Toscanini said.

Marian Anderson has never sung under the baton of this great maestro; but she did sing under Bruno Walter's direction in Vienna, the alto solo part in Brahms's "Alt Rhapsody." She had been engaged for only one performance and had not studied this long and difficult part without the score. At the rehearsal, she sang with the music in her hand. After the orchestra left, Bruno Walter went through the composition at the piano with her. He even sang the part for Marian, not so much to instruct her as to let her see that he could do it without the score.

As he said, "Good-by until tomorrow," he added, "When one sings under my direction, she does not use a score."

Marian smiled a little and left the hall. When we arrived at our hotel, she began at once to rehearse the part and in a most decided voice said to me, "I shall sing the part tomorrow without the score." We worked on it late in the evening and again early in the morning; and when the concert took place, Marian walked calmly in and stood in her place in front of the orchestra without the score. This brought an astonished but pleased look from Mr. Walter. And when Miss Anderson, without making any mistakes, finished the difficult Brahms rhapsody, he reached out his hand and gave her a hearty handshake.

A word about the applause Miss Anderson receives. No doubt nothing makes an artist happier than to receive much applause from the audience. It testifies that the whole audience is appreciative and is with the artist heart and soul.

An artist is deeply moved, for instance, when an audience of young college or high school students receives him with intense applause. This sort of audience loudly clap their young, strong hands, often even stamp their feet to show their youthful enthusiasm in a fierce hurricane of sound.

But silence, in my opinion, can often mean the greatest applause of all. No doubt there are very few artists living who can create in a concert hall a feeling of reverence and silence. Marian Anderson has a few times received this unusual kind of applause. Each time it was after she sang the Negro spiritual "Crucifixion," arranged by Payne.

This kind of applause can be expected only of a highly cultured audience, of course. And this is the kind of applause Marian received here in Salzburg. After her rendition of "Crucifixion" the distinguished audience sat in utter silence. No one moved. I hardly dared to close the music and open the next song, and when I finally did so my hand was trembling.

Marian stood silent, with half-closed eyes, for some time. Then she moved her head slowly toward me, opened her eyes, gave a little smile, closed her eyes again, and began to sing the next number. (I might explain here that while singing Miss Anderson always closes her eyes.)

The same thing had happened twice before this,

ON THE STAGE OF THE MOZARTEUM, SALZBURG (MR. VEHANEN
AT THE PIANO).

MARIAN ANDERSON WITH HER ITALIAN TEACHER, MME. GENI SADERO,
AT VILLA SIRIUS, CAP FERRAT, ON THE RIVIERA.

both times in Scandinavia and under somewhat different conditions. The first time was in a church in Finland. (There, incidentally, pianos are never used in churches, and we were obliged to use the organ for the accompaniments. Scandinavian people are deeply religious.)

The second time was in a church in a little Swedish city. Here a piano was used, but no applause was permitted. Instead of the clapping of hands, the audience raised their handkerchiefs at arm's length and waved them as a sign of appreciation. It is often quite as agreeable to the performing artist to face a sea of white, waving handkerchiefs in a large hall as it is to hear loud applause.

In the Swedish church, when Miss Anderson sang "Crucifixion," however, not a handkerchief was waved; no one felt like lifting his hand. Instead, the audience sat quiet and used their handkerchiefs to wipe away the tears that fell upon their cheeks.

BEFORE I GO FURTHER, I MUST RE-
late some episodes in my career before I met Miss
Anderson. In Europe, I had the good fortune of
working with two of the most eminent concert
singers of our time.

The first was Mme. Charles Cahier, an Ameri-
can-born singer, a perfect musician, with excellent
style in German songs. She was contralto prima
donna in the Vienna and the Munich opera houses.
There she had the opportunity to sing under one
of the greatest composers and conductors, Gustav
Mahler. In him, she had a marvelous friend who
guided her in the interpretation of German songs.
During the five years I was with her, in which we

[137]

presented from five to six hundred recitals, I learned from her the exact style of interpreting especially the songs of Hugo Wolf and Gustav Mahler, and also many other German lieder composers. Mme. Cahier had the great courage to put on her programs, along with the great names, those of young, talented composers.

During the time I have known her, Miss Anderson has studied in Europe for only short periods, during which she usually combined her vacations with work. I told Marian about my old friend Mme. Cahier and suggested that Marian study a group of Gustav Mahler's songs with her. Mme. Cahier was spending her vacation that year in Jáchymov, a little resort in Czechoslovakia famous for its radium treatments. She had a class of five or six pupils, which Marian joined. The class was held in an unused school building outside the city. We enjoyed our stay there because of the exceptional peace and solitude of the surroundings. Under the tutorship of this brilliant woman, Marian soon added a group of Mahler's songs to her repertoire.

Our little vacation had a strange ending, however. The day after Marian and I left Jáchymov, some policemen and detectives came to the hotel to search Mme. Cahier's room. This, of course, upset her, and she asked the reason for the search. Unable to find anything wrong, they were obliged to offer apologies to Mme. Cahier, explaining that someone had accused her and her pupils, including me, of being connected with a gang of smugglers. We were supposed to be directed by Mme. Cahier. I, apparently the head smuggler, was said to have brought into the country three thousand pairs of stockings. The whole story was stupid, to say the least. They said that I carried the goods in a big drum and instructed the pupils to sell the stockings. Everyone knew that I was not a drum player and certainly never carried a drum around with me.

The details of this incident had become part of the official records, however, and this caused Marian and me some trouble when we later made a tour of Czechoslovakia. It was such an inconvenience that we were forced to ask the authorities at the Finnish legation to handle the case and see that we got new visas. We eventually got them with profuse apologies.

Another teacher who contributed in no small measure to Miss Anderson's art was Mme. Germaine de Castro. Under her tutorship, Miss Anderson studied the French language and songs.

This teacher, who develops an exceptionally clear French diction, was eager to teach Marian, and the arrangement proved very satisfactory both in the language lessons and in improving Marian's voice. The voice became much more flexible and gained in clarity. It is the tendency of most Negro singers to sing the septime too low, but under Mme. de Castro's guidance this tendency almost disappeared.

While studying with Mme. de Castro, Miss Anderson rented a villa on the Riviera between Nice and Monte Carlo. Here she enjoyed nature immensely and expressed the wish to purchase a house and live on the blue Mediterranean during all her vacations.

The house she then had was large, with the music studio on the ground floor next to the garage. This particular location was advantageous, because we could work undisturbed, and Mme. de Castro and Marian studied on an average of three times a day, with marvelous results.

Some readers are, no doubt, curious as to how Miss Anderson studies new songs. There are no secrets; there are no extraordinary methods—simply a sound approach to each song. First of all, I choose a number of songs that I feel will fit properly into a particular program. We then select one group of these, and I play them for her. We consider how the songs will go together and arrange them in a tentative program before we actually know any of the songs. We read the poetry through carefully; no matter how good the music may be, Marian rejects a song if the poetry isn't to her liking.

Then we begin to study one song after another. During the first week Miss Anderson sings a song an octave lower than it is written, so that if you were listening, you would surely believe that it was a man singing. The coaching, too, in this stage is only a rhythmical playing of the song over and over. When the technical part is well learned, Marian takes the music, goes into her bedroom, and memorizes the words. On the following day, or the day after, when the melody and the words are memorized, we begin the real creation of the songs.

I remember one time when I was at Roland Hayes's home and we were going over some songs for our own amusement, I was surprised at a rubato that he introduced into a Schubert song. He explained that he does not try to sing even Schubert songs as others sing them; he likes to find his own beauties in every song. It is this type of studying that Miss Anderson has always endeavored to do. She attempts to find, not the traditional way to perform songs but the *characteristic* way, the way that satisfies the ideal of beauty and dramatic feeling that she has in her heart.

This is the key to the creations of Marian Anderson. They are very personal, often very strange, but always true to her inner feeling. It is necessary to know traditions and dangerous for singers who are not creators to go beyond them. But for singers of Miss Anderson's quality, a tradition is only a steppingstone to the creation of her own beauty.

When the songs are approximately ready, we rehearse the whole recital program with full voice just as she sings it on the concert stage. Then, if necessary, we change the order of some songs, sometimes replacing one song with another.

The program is the result of very careful study from the beginning to the final stages, and the result has been, in most cases, first-class, balanced programs.

On the Riviera, Marian had a most agreeable servant, a French girl named Colombine, who prepared very appetizing French food. Each day, as she served the meals, she would tell us that the food contained some special, natural curative power. One day the food was good for the liver, the next day for the heart, another for the kidneys, and so on.

Marian began to acquire epicurean tastes. On first arriving in Europe, Marian was inclined to refuse dishes she had not been accustomed to, preferring those of her native land; but after tasting the delicacies of the French and Swedish tables, such as snails, a special preparation of oysters, *plätter* (a Swedish pancake), and others, she became less insistent about American food and really began to like European cooking. The European manner of using the knife and fork at first seemed strange to Marian, but after a while it became more natural to her, and she no longer ate with her left hand under the table.

Colombine made a great effort to please Miss Anderson. When we got up from the table, if we appeared well satisfied and if every plate was empty, Colombine would always give a happy smile, feeling that she had pleased us.

On the Riviera, we met many interesting people. One day Princess Arfa came as a guest to one of Miss Anderson's excellent dinners. The princess was born a Finn, and she had married a Persian prince. She was once a slender beauty but now had become quite a large woman. She was extremely cultivated, a striking personality. She had spent twenty-five years in her harem in Constantinople. Being now a widow, she had left the harem and lived in her castle on the Riviera, in Monte Carlo.

As a young girl, Princess Arfa had been a newspaper writer in Helsinki. She told us a charming story about our mutual friend Sibelius. On a Christmas morning, she was standing in front of a flower shop as Sibelius came along. He stopped and told her that her last article was so beautifully written that it inspired him to write a new composition. He gallantly made a gesture toward the window, saying, "All these flowers belong to you." Then he went into the store with the intention of buying all the roses for her—but he came out, alas, with only one rose. As he gave her the flower, he said, "I am very sorry that I didn't have more money with me."

Marian listened to the princess's stories of the harem and of the old life in Constantinople with intense interest. She told us about the harem wives and girls and the high servant, dressed in gay elegance with silks and precious stones, with a sword at his side. He was the important man who took care of the many birds in the harem.

Our stay on the beautiful Riviera was all too short, and Marian looked forward to her return. Many plans were made and wishes expressed, but, as so often happens, the next summer never came.

Another singer who indirectly helped in the preparation of Miss Anderson's programs was Helge Lindberg, the famous Finnish baritone. He had played a big part in my musical experience before I met Miss Anderson. He died at only forty years of age, shortly after he had signed a contract for his first American concert tour—which explains why his name is not better known in this country. He was the foremost Bach and Handel exponent of our time. Mr. Lindberg possessed a very strong artistic bent and went his own way in everything. The programs he gave were always heavy, and he never changed them to please the managers or the public; in other words, he did just what he wanted to do.

I recall that when he first sang in Paris with the famous Colonne Orchestra, he had three unknown Handel arias on his program. The conductor refused to do the program as it was, saying no singer had ever done this in Paris before. Mr. Lindberg simply answered, "I sing what I choose or not at all." This made the conductor curious, and he asked Mr. Lindberg to sing the arias for him privately, which he did. After hearing them, the conductor at once accepted the original program.

Mr. Lindberg searched diligently through museums and libraries to find unpublished manuscripts of the classics and found many exquisite numbers, which he included in his repertoire. One of his most famous numbers was Bach's "Kreutzstab Cantata," and he presented many of the same composer's secular cantatas. For his interest in and interpretations of Bach's music he was made an honorary member of many Bach societies.

I had spoken to Miss Anderson many times about this artist. She was greatly interested and expressed the desire to become better acquainted with the kind of songs he sang. When the time seemed right and I saw that her desire was serious, I suggested that we look up Mr. Lindberg's own collection.

His widow, an artist in her own right, was kind enough to promise to let me use everything from her late husband's library. At this time, she was on a world tour with a variety show, but their old home in Vienna, which had been untouched, was open to me.

During Miss Anderson's first visit to Vienna, I secured the key to my old friend's apartment. It was a strange feeling that came over me when I opened the door of my friend's home to see on the wall directly in front of me a grinning mask—a piece of sculpture that he had made, under which he had inscribed the words, "Again a guest."

Thick layers of dust covered everything. I looked into his bedroom, and I caressed the old piano, as fond memories surged through my mind. I could scarcely begin to go through his large collection of music in search of songs that would be suitable for Marian's voice. However, as I continued to work with the dusty music, I found some beautiful and rare songs with the fingering that I had marked years ago.

When I brought this large bundle of music to Marian, she took it and, pressing it close to her breast, cried joyfully, "Now I know him at last."

From this moment Miss Anderson's love for this old and beloved repertoire began, and she had the earnest desire to sing great and rare songs.

Another source of songs for Miss Anderson's programs was the following. While Marian and I were on vacation, she sent me to Zurich, Switzerland, to study in Hug's music store, where I knew the finest collection of music in Europe was to be found. With the help of Mr. Otto Moser, a man of incomparable musical knowledge, I sat for hours and hours, playing through everything, and finding many precious songs.

With what I found from these sources, Miss Anderson now has a first-class collection of music, from which we can choose exquisite compositions almost without limit for her recitals.

THE WELL-KNOWN MUSICIAN AND author, John Erskine, wrote not long ago, "The quality of music which Marian Anderson has sung has been of the highest, and after her programs anything less fine seems cheap indeed. To help raise the taste of a whole people in any one field of art is a privilege only the most fortunate educators enjoy. I rank Marian Anderson among the most fortunate."

But it took a very long time to produce these first-class programs. It is well known that ten or fifteen years ago an ideal American program was made up to include as many composers' names as possible. The average person has gone far in musical education, however, and we now find, more often than not, well-arranged recital programs given during the concert season. Even today one meets with objections if one sings an entire program of songs by a single composer. For this reason most artists prefer to have several different composers represented.

The German programs of about twenty years ago went to the other extreme. A program of one composer's work was quite stylish and a Schubert, a Brahms, or a Hugo Wolf evening, quite the fashion. Although I do not wish to imply that these programs were monotonous, it seems to me that for a singer of the highest attainments they are not suitable. To maintain her supremacy in the concert world, the great singer must have all the colors in her artistic spectrum visible. It is not very easy to accomplish this with songs exclusively by one composer.

When Miss Anderson arrived in Europe, her programs were conceived in typical American form. A number of composers, some quite unimportant, were on them. Miss Anderson's first coach in Berlin suggested many other songs in an effort to acquaint the newcomer with different types.

The first programs in Scandinavia did not include

MISS ANDERSON IN PARIS.

all the kinds of songs audiences there had been accustomed to hear. Most visiting artists had many songs in German, French, and Italian on their programs. The absence of these on Miss Anderson's programs was conspicuous. But her voice carried all before it.

I do not think that I am very wrong if I say that Miss Anderson is most decidedly a Handel-Schubert singer. The clear, sustained, beautiful melodies and the deep tragic feeling in the Handel and Schubert songs are most congenial to her voice and character. If Marian Anderson were a composer, I am sure she would write in the style of these composers.

One time, in speaking with me about Marian's programs, Jean Sibelius said, "You have excellent taste, and I believe, as you do, that the last century was a Bach century and our century is to be Handel's."

Handel's compositions have proved to be among Miss Anderson's most admired and effective interpretations.

If there is a fault in her programs it is perhaps the operatic aria, which still remains as a leftover from former days. This, however, is not Miss Anderson's fault, nor is it mine, but it is a fault of those who believe that the program of a great artist is somehow not complete without an operatic number of some kind.

Marian Anderson's ideas about modern music are very decided; she definitely dislikes disagreeable sounds and unclear harmonies. She feels that in this kind of music there is a sort of sickness that is the result of our troubled times and that has put its seal on our music, drama, painting, literature, and architecture.

In another respect, her viewpoint is in complete harmony with mine: we do not enjoy atonal music, where a thousand badly written notes could be replaced with ten well-written ones.

In reference to her singing of Negro spirituals, there have been varied opinions. That she loves these songs is indubitable. They are songs that still echo in her soul from childhood memories, and religion is the core of Marian Anderson's life philosophy. She sings these songs more from a spiritual standpoint than does any other Negro singer. She follows the Negro tradition in that, at a recital, in a moment of ecstasy, she often changes the written melody, inserting a note or two of improvisation. She emphasizes not the childish naïveté in these songs, as some singers do, but their deep religious feeling.

Both Roland Hayes and Paul Robeson interpret them from another viewpoint. It is not necessary to say that one is right and the other wrong. But I still think that Miss Anderson's interpretation of Negro spirituals stands on a very high level. The Negro spiritual "Crucifixion" is one of her best songs; it brings out the fantastic colors and the velvety texture of her voice, and the touching words have a meaning for all mankind. But she reaches the highest artistic climax in Schubert's "Ave Maria" or "Doppelgänger," in Schumann's "Ich grolle nicht," in Handel's "Begrüssung" or "Der Flöte weich," in Bach's "Kom' süsser Tod," and many others.

One criticism sometimes made about Miss Anderson's programs is that she does not include more light, joyful numbers at her recitals. I compare those who ask such a question to people who inquire of the director of the Metropolitan Opera Company why Lily Pons does not sing the role of Carmen; or why Kirsten Flagstad doesn't sing Mignon; or Martinelli, the role of the toreador. The very moment an artist goes outside the limit of his resources and character, he is lost.

[155]

Eleonora Duse and Sarah Bernhardt did occasionally play comic roles, however, although their reputations were made by their acting of tragedy. In the films, the same can be said about Greta Garbo.

Miss Anderson uses as extra numbers a few lighter songs, such as Liza Lehmann's "Cuckoo," which she sings in a genial manner and interprets with assurance. But the greatness of Marian Anderson lies in the rendition of tragic lieder.

Another extra number, called "Obstination," is by Bianchini. Marian and I met this composer in Venice, where one rides to a recital in a gondola. Mr. Bianchini gave us the manuscript of "Obstination" when Miss Anderson had a world success singing it. He wanted to publish it, but there was a reason why he did not do so at the time. The exquisite words of the song were written by an extremely fat lady who always received her guests lying in her bed. Her face was very beautiful, but she was always covered with a tiger skin. No one ever saw her standing erect. When the question of publishing the song was considered, it was, of course, necessary to get the permission of this lady. So Mr. Bianchini went to Paris, where she was living. But he was never able to find her. The beautiful face and the tiger skin had disappeared, no one knew where, and the song could not be published. The composer waited for four years, and when he was unable to locate the lady, published the song at his own risk.

In speaking of Miss Anderson's programs, I humbly mention my own songs. I recall a charming Finnish folk melody that I arranged for her as an extra number. I did this with no pretensions, at the time, of being a composer. It is a song full of color and serves its purpose well. At her first recital in New York, the song had such success that it had to be sung twice.

The following day the Galaxy Music Company's director, Mr. Walter Kramer, asked if this song had been published. I answered, "No, it has not. It is not even in manuscript; it is only in my mind."

He requested me to write it and said he would be glad to publish it, which he did.

Then I began to compose other songs, of varied character, to be used on Marian Anderson's programs. Composing these songs gave me real enjoyment. It had always been easy for me to write poems, and now I found that it was equally easy for me to fit those poems to music.

This work gave an added charm to my life, and

I am indebted to Mr. Kramer and certainly grateful to Miss Anderson. They were the means of my becoming a composer.

Marian Anderson strives to make the recordings of her voice sound as natural and perfect in every detail as possible. This takes much study and patience as well as experience. She does not want her voice to sound smaller or bigger than it sounds when she is singing normally.

Many voices heard on records and on the radio are, of course, not of the highest quality. One also very often hears records in which it is impossible to find the climax in a song. This quite often is the fault not of the singers but of the studio technicians.

It is a well-known fact that Miss Anderson's voice comes over the air waves beautifully and naturally. But making a recording is quite different. An excellent recording of a voice depends not only on the artist but also on the studio engineers. This is true of radio, too, though apparently not to so great an extent.

When Marian has an appointment with a recording studio, she always keeps it to the minute. Sometimes her stay is not long. If she feels, after singing the first song, that she is not up to par, she explains that she will make no more recordings that day. It doesn't matter if the studio director says, "Oh, that was beautiful." Miss Anderson follows strictly her own feeling in the matter. When she is at her best, she sings six songs in one visit to the recording studio, but seldom more.

A few years ago, in Paris, she received the first prize for making the best record of the year for "His Master's Voice" Company—"Death and the Maiden," by Schubert.

Not all her records that are on the market entirely satisfy Marian. Some she feels are not her very best, though the majority are excellent. The reason that a few of them are not her best is that they were released without her personal O.K. at times when she was touring the country or abroad.

Miss Anderson, I believe, does her best singing when she has a large audience. I refer here to the radio broadcast as well as the concert stage. An empty radio or recording studio is not always conducive to the best results in her singing.

JUST AS MISS ANDERSON'S DEVELOP-
ment from a good singer to a world-famous artist
was most amazing, so also was the rapid change in
her ideas about dress. Whereas earlier she had been
content with dresses of simpler style, she now chose
gowns in finer taste and of a more exclusive design.

Even as a young accompanist, I was always very
much interested in the kind of gowns my soloists
wore at recitals. The famous prima donna of the
great Paris Opera, Aïno Ackté, for whom I was
accompanist, would always ask me to go to her
clothes closet and choose a gown for her to wear at
her recitals. Once I chose one that she had worn in
the second act of "Romeo and Juliet"; so you see

that my taste in the beginning was not so very good.

But when I met Miss Anderson, I had already learned more about proper dress and styles. At first she wore plain dresses without trains, and her favorite color was blue. I recall also a dress that she had brought to Europe from America, of white satin, close-fitting, without trimming or color.

Once, when her bag was open slightly, I got a glimpse of a piece of cardinal red material, and I wondered what it was. (In those days I was not allowed to pack or have anything to do with her luggage; she was displeased if anyone attempted to look into her bags, and they were usually kept closed.) I asked her what that lovely red material was, and she reluctantly told me that it was a cape to be worn with the white satin dress.

"For heaven's sake, why don't you wear it? That color should be most effective."

"No, I cannot wear it on the stage. It is too much."

"Don't you like it?" I queried.

"Yes, I like it very well."

When I insisted day after day that she wear the lovely red cape, she finally mustered up enough courage and wore it once. It created a fine effect on the audience, and she began wearing it more often.

In my imagination, I always thought that her tall, slender figure ought to be draped in a formal gown with a train. But Marian would always say, "No train. I shall never wear a train. I cannot walk easily if I have a train on my gowns."

When we were in Stockholm, I again tried to persuade her, and she at last purchased a very attractive gown with a small train. I was pleased and thought that my coaxing was now over. But at the second recital at which she wore this gown, the train was no longer to be seen; she had cut it off with her scissors.

In private life, she wore very simple dresses.

I shall never forget the first hat I saw on her, in Berlin. Older clothes are undoubtedly comfortable. But when I saw the same hat worn again and again in all Miss Anderson's photographs, I decided that it must disappear. Just how I was not sure.

I was very seldom in Miss Anderson's room, and when she was out of her room she always wore the hat. Of course, I could not snatch it off her head.

At last the opportunity came. We were rehearsing in a room in our hotel, and the little upright piano that I used stood diagonally in one corner.

When Marian rehearses, she always takes off her hat. This time she placed it on top of the piano, and when I saw her turn her back toward me, I quickly shoved the hat out of sight into the corner behind the piano.

When it was time to leave, Marian looked for her hat, asking, "Didn't I have my hat when I came in?"

"No, I didn't see it," I answered quickly.

I could feel her trying to look directly into my eyes, but I did not pay much attention to what she said or did and purposely got busy packing my music. She made an exhaustive inquiry around the hotel about her hat, but it was never found.

I tried to console her by saying that someone must have taken it as a sort of souvenir or remembrance. The strange thing is that when forced to buy a new one, she not only bought one but continued to get one right after another. She never blamed me for losing the old hat; she never dreamed that I was the mischievous, guilty one.

The first really elegant gowns that Miss Anderson purchased were from the N.K., an exclusive and beautiful store in Stockholm where the latest Paris models were to be found. One of the most attractive gowns was a brilliant black lace entirely embroidered with black pearls.

At this time she always carried a handkerchief with her on the stage. At the recital where she wore the black lace gown, she carried a large, expensive lace handkerchief that someone had given her. Marian seemed to have an idea that her hands looked too large, and she would try to cover them with the handkerchief as she stood on the stage, ready to sing. (Actually, Miss Anderson's hands are very well formed and expressive.) When the people in the audience noticed that she liked handkerchiefs, they began to send her one after another. The first ones she had used were small and inexpensive, but now they grew in size until no larger ones were to be found. Then she stopped carrying any at all.

After the first dress, however, Marian never again cut the trains from her gowns. Instead, she began to wear longer ones.

In Vienna, Miss Anderson met a man who really knew how to design clothes to her liking—Professor Ladislaus Czettel, who designed the most exclusive models for her, from which she would select the ones that appealed to her most.

The first gown Professor Czettel created for Miss Anderson was of white satin, beautiful in design, with a very long train; around the shoulders was a large scarf of the same material, which could be draped in two or three different ways. This Miss Anderson liked better than any of her other recital gowns.

Professor Czettel not only designed her concert gowns but made a whole new wardrobe for her. From that moment, she was a well-dressed woman of excellent taste.

In this connection I must mention Marian's jewelry. The first piece that I remember was a gold ring that resembled a school or a college ring. However, she soon had the desire to wear more brilliant jewels. We often looked in the stores and shops for something new that might please her and be suitable to wear.

One day, as I was window-shopping in Stockholm, I discovered a magnificent diamond brooch in a jewelry store. I urged Marian to go to see it, for I was sure it was an extraordinary and rare piece.

Marian and I went together to look at it. As she was admiring it, the clerk told us that it contained three hundred diamonds and had been designed and made in France in about 1850 for a Swedish king to present to his mistress. The brooch had been placed on sale because the family of the mistress needed money. It was priced at a large amount, but Marian purchased it at once anyway.

Slowly her collection grew until she had many beautiful pieces of jewelry. Among them are large baroque pearls bought in Russia, clear, limpid aquamarines, extremely dark amethysts, turquoise bracelets, and a large topaz ring of exquisite color and beauty. But she seldom wears any of them. She wears daily an unusual diamond ring, which, in design and workmanship, looks as though it could have come from her ancestral Africa.

In Paris, Miss Anderson's dressmaker was Molyneux, and here the gown which she wore at her recital at the Paris Opera was created. It was golden lamé, extremely fine and soft, with long, tight sleeves. When she appeared in this brilliant gown, with the diamond brooch and the topaz ring, in the golden surroundings of L'Opéra, no one could believe that this statuesque woman was the same young girl who, four years previously,

[167]

had cut the little train off her gown as she said, "That's too much."

But the miracle revealed at the Paris Opera was not only in the outer appearance but also in Miss Anderson's art. It was no longer merely wonderful singing but real creation. She understood the deepest meaning of the words and delivered them in such a way that everyone could grasp their significance. The reading of the poetry was perfect, and the languages were without accent. The incorrect sounding of the English letters "l" and "t" had disappeared. Even the most difficult language, French, was now clear as crystal. When the director of the Paris Opera, in evening clothes and high hat, greeted Miss Anderson during the intermission, he assured her that her diction was worthy of the finest traditions of the French language at L'Opéra.

The diamond brooch played a part in a strange occurrence at one of the two recitals we gave in the Paris Opera. As we left our rooms at the hotel for the recital, Marian motioned, as she always does before closing her door, with her upturned fingers as a good-by to her room. We went down the long corridor to the self-operating elevator and

MISS ANDERSON IN GOWN WORN AT THE PARIS OPERA.

rang the bell. The car came up slowly, and through the glass door we could see the form of an old woman. I opened the door and waited for her to come out, but she didn't move. Her glassy eyes stared at Marian's diamond brooch. Her whole face was made up; her withered thin lips looked like a red line; her eyelids were dark blue. Around her thin neck, she wore a string of imitation pearls; and she wore a hat suitable for a girl of eighteen. She leaned on her cane and made no move, although her eyes were still on the diamonds. I had a feeling that this was a ghost, not a human being.

At last she began to take small steps toward the door. Marian and I looked at each other, feeling disturbed; and as she stepped out of the elevator, we quickly entered and went down.

As the old-fashioned lift stopped at the main floor, we again saw through the glass door the form of an old woman. The door opened, and in front of us stood a much-wrinkled woman of about ninety. There was no make-up on her face. She also had eyes only for the diamonds. She stood in such a way as to prevent us from leaving the elevator, and I felt like brushing her to one side but did not dare to, since she was so very aged that I was afraid she would fall. Finally, one of the hall men came and guided her aside so that we could get out, but she kept turning her head to see Marian.

I told Marian she had better go back to her room and say good-by over again, for two ghosts appearing just before a recital would bring ill luck. Marian and I are both superstitious. "Do you really think it will bring bad luck?" Marian asked.

"Yes, I believe it will," I answered. "Just as you believe that you shouldn't put a sharp instrument in anyone's hand or say good-by under a doorway, so I definitely feel that you should go back to your room and start all over again."

"Oh, you are being childish; they are only two old women, and we haven't much time," Marian said. So we took our taxi and drove to L'Opéra.

The car brought us through the well-kept courtyard of this marvelous building to the door of the stage entrance, where there is another glass door. Through this, I was surprised to see once again the form of an old woman. As we entered, we saw this time an old, well-dressed woman, who resembled a prima donna of about sixty years ago. Her blue eyes shimmered with belladonna; the gray silk dress rustled around her, and on her head was a hat trimmed with lavender lilacs. With a friendly but artificial smile, she greeted Marian, her blue eyes glued on the diamond brooch. As we walked up the stairs to the dressing room on the second floor, we could hear the rattling silk behind us. As soon as we entered, the door was closed.

We never again saw any of the three women, but we did have a further occasion to remember them.

In the artists' room, Marian was, as always, calm, never fearing that anything out of the ordinary would happen. Another artist might have taken a drink, but she never uses stimulants and is not nervous. Clear water and some warm, weak tea are all she ever takes. Soon to face the most brilliant and exacting audience in the whole world, perhaps, she showed no trace of nervousness.

Where does this great surety in her singing and her appearance come from? What makes it possible, for instance, for her to take as her first note in a recital the first note in Handel's "Begrüssung," which is twenty-seven seconds long, with no vibration or shaking in the voice?

Stage fright, in my opinion, exists when an artist is not sure of her technique, memory, or health, which are, of course, most important. An artist who is very sure of herself in these points never experiences stage fright. No doubt every artist is more or less excited; and it is quite necessary to be excited, for this makes the person feel keyed up emotionally, more sensitive and able to catch the right expression. But Marian Anderson has other forces that help her—the unusual balance of her character and the fact that she can face every situation with a strong spiritual faith. In every move, she is confident that God directs and guides her in the way that is best.

She is blessed with physical fortitude, too. For instance, her average pulse is fifty-five, whereas the normal pulse is seventy-two. It is quite interesting to know that Napoleon's pulse was fifty-three; and the pulse of the great Finnish runner, Paavo Nurmi, is fifty-four. When Miss Anderson is a little nervous, it disturbs her breathing in no way, and her pulse remains reasonably slow.

We stood behind the rostrum, ready to go on the stage; the door was opened, and Marian took three steps on the stage and quickly backed off again. The view that confronted her took her off her feet. The gorgeousness of this famous house, the brilliant lighting effects, the stunningly dressed people all had a powerful effect on her. As she stepped back from the stage, she put her hand to her brow, pushing at her hair. Then she took a deep breath and walked slowly onto the stage again. One who has never stood upon this stage facing an audience of gaily gowned, diamond-bedecked Parisian ladies and gentlemen in their evening clothes cannot easily imagine the sparkling and festive sight.

When I was about to start to play, I hesitated, feeling that this sight was so very beautiful and inspiring that no music was necessary to augment it. Marian sang with the full artistry of which she was capable. On the program was, of course, Schubert's "Ave Maria." The first crescendo on the word "Maria" was so very touching and filled with beauty, that even I lifted my eyes in admiration; and as I did so I noticed that the three large diamonds in the lower part of Marian's brooch seemed to stand straight up as if by magic. For the moment, however, I was so much absorbed in the lovely singing that I quite forgot about the diamonds.

At the finish of this glorious recital, Marian looked in her dressing-room mirror and to her great astonishment discovered that the three large diamonds in her brooch were missing. (The brooch was made so that certain parts could be taken out and used as earrings.) At once every door was closed and the search begun. The stage was covered with a thin carpet, and there was no way for the diamonds to fall down through the stage. The footlights were examined. But after a long search, not one diamond had been found. The following day, a more thorough search was made, but all in vain.

"Why didn't you go back to your room at the hotel when we saw the first ghost?" I said to Marian. "We saw three, and you lost three diamonds."

Marian believed then that what I had advised her at the beginning was right.

But what is it to lose three diamonds when you win the diadem of a queen among the singers of the world? What Australia gave in Melba, Italy, in Caruso, Germany, in Schumann-Heink, Russia, in Chaliapin, the United States has given in Marian Anderson.

ON OUR SECOND VISIT TO BARCE-
lona, Spain, in 1936, the room clerk in our hotel
asked us one evening what we would like to eat
the next day. A strange question, we thought, for
a large hotel, but the explanation was very simple:
"Tomorrow is Labor Day. No one is working;
there will be no cooking; so we must ask our guests
what kind of cold meal they would like."

There were much confusion and excitement in
the streets, which were crowded with people. I
could see the dark expression in many faces and a
fanatic look in many eyes. I had had the same kind
of feeling in Finland before the Russian revolution.

The next day, Marian and I were invited for

luncheon at the home of the famous Spanish singer Conchita Badia. As I looked out my window in the morning, I could see great throngs of people carrying red flags as they marched through the streets. Not a taxicab was visible. It was apparent that everyone was celebrating the holiday and no one working. How should Marian and I get to our friend's home? This was the question.

As it happened, a government official was also invited to the luncheon. He graciously telephoned us saying that he would send a government car for us. When we stepped out the hotel door, the car was waiting, but we were quite surprised when we noticed, just behind our car, another one filled with policemen. We were among the few in Barcelona that day who were privileged to drive in a car; but our government official told us later that it would have been dangerous even for him to drive through the streets without an escort.

At the luncheon Marian and I met many very interesting Spanish artists. We had music and a marvelous time, but over all the joy there seemed to be a dark shadow lurking.

I was the only person present who had had the experience of going through a communist revolution; and I was the only one whose home had been demolished by those cruel people. So of course I felt keenly the seriousness of the situation.

I held a long political conversation with the high government official. I had a feeling that he did not regard the present confusion seriously enough. To me it seemed as though he were discussing a chess game with ivory pieces as counters, not human beings.

Before leaving, I told him, "I don't think you quite realize the great force of the masses when they begin to move."

"We have a strong government," he answered. "Don't you fear. First we shall enjoy Miss Anderson's art; then we make a little revolution." And he gave a bright, forced laugh.

To this day I can plainly see his smiling face. But, alas, it is now only a death mask, for he was one of the first to be executed in the Spanish civil war.

The next day we were to leave for Valencia, but there were no trains running; so we were forced to obtain a private motorcar to drive us to our destination. Since the chauffeur did not dare to leave Barcelona in the daytime, we pulled out from the city just before dawn. The roads curved high up

[179]

into the mountains and afforded us a splendid view out over the Mediterranean. Once again we had a feeling of peace, enjoyed nature, and took deep breaths of relief. As we drew near Valencia, the road led down to the yellow sea sand, and the soil looked more cultivated. Ripe oranges were hanging on the dark-leaved trees. The road was bordered for miles with roses, and the atmosphere was perfumed with blossoms of all kinds.

In Valencia, the excitement was again evident, with nervous-looking people surging around as though expecting a terrible thunderstorm. Policemen were numerous and strongly on the watch. In Madrid, the uprising had already reached great heights.

At the crowded railroad station, we wanted something to eat. But it was almost impossible to get into the restaurant. After a short wait, we found a table just inside the door. The waiter, who was excited, hardly heard what we ordered; and when he brought the food, he fairly threw it on the table.

It looked as though all the people were carrying their belongings through the streets, but no one seemed to know just why or where he was going, and the cries of women and children filled the air.

The only one who remained unexcited was Marian; and she decided to go on and give her recital in Bilbao.

We were indeed greatly relieved when our car started out for the border near San Sebastian. Here we were ordered by customs officers to have our luggage examined. One of the first things that they saw was Marian's elegant evening cape, which she had purchased in Moscow and which was originally a pope's cape. It was of dark red velvet, trimmed with rich silver and gold embroidery.

"What is this?" he gruffly asked.

"That is Miss Anderson's evening cape," I quickly answered.

"And do you think that I believe that this girl wears evening capes as gorgeous as this one?"

"Anyway, it is true," I exclaimed. "This girl is a famous singer and often uses this cape on the way to her recitals."

"Doesn't she have any other capes besides those that are stolen from churches?"

"Stolen?" I asked. "I don't understand what you mean."

"I mean stolen. We just had a telegram from headquarters to be on the lookout for such things

[181]

here at the border. You shall both be detained," he said loudly.

I quickly recalled that we had with us some photographs of Miss Anderson wearing this very cape. She had had them taken in Stockholm about a year before. We found the pictures and showed them to the customs officer. He then began to understand and excused us. We happily packed the beautiful evening cape in the trunk again and left the customhouse.

As we came over the border into France, we both looked sadly back, thinking of poor, beautiful Spain and the terrible future she was facing. This charming country, with perfumes of oranges and sweet roses, still lingers in our minds.

IT IS NOW TEN MINUTES TO FOUR, and Miss Anderson has gone shopping. It is nearly time for you to leave for South America."

"Then we shall probably be late."

"Yes . . . probably."

This was a conversation between the clerk in the Majestic Hotel in Cannes and myself.

Marian had been late for sailings before. On the eve of our first voyage from New York to South America, Marian gave a supper party, after which I escorted her home. I went up to her apartment to get my boat ticket, which she had. I was astonished to see that nothing was packed; all the twenty-five trunks lay scattered about the floor, empty, and the closets were still filled with her gowns. I saw at once that she would be quite unable to pack alone, so I stayed to help her. We worked steadily all night, and at about 5 A.M. everything was ready; but where were the tickets? We looked in vain, then started to unpack. Finally Marian found them between hundreds of unopened letters in a large sack. At last we were ready to leave for our steamer.

Many times we have missed trains. I remember that once we arrived at the railroad station in Paris an hour after our train had left. The porters stared at us as though we were crazy.

But in Cannes she was on time. She arrived at two minutes to four with her secretary, who was loaded down with packages of all sizes. All the people at the hotel were anxious for us; only Marian was calmly smiling. Our car was waiting at the door. We jumped in and rushed to the pier. Upon arriving there we were told that our liner was half an hour late, which we were glad to hear, since this gave us a little breathing spell.

The wind was strong, and the small tender that took us out to the liner tossed around like a floating log.

Marian, who is never fond of sea trips, said to me, "Why didn't I come *too* late?"

But everything was all right after we boarded the large *Augustus* for our second South American tour. There was a brilliant sun, and the wind was still very fresh as we moved out and headed for Gibraltar. A large Italian flag was spread on the deck, the only sign of dangerous times. The civil war was going on in Spain, and our boat was obliged to stay far out from the Spanish coast. With curiosity, we looked for some signs of war, but nothing exciting happened. As we neared Gibraltar, large pillars of smoke were plainly visible, but we were never sure where they originated.

We eagerly looked forward to the famous seaport Dakar, where our *Augustus* was to stop for a supply of oil. Watching from the deck, we caught our first glimpse of Africa—Marian's ancestral Africa, which, for a long time, she had dreamed of seeing.

Arriving in Dakar at about four in the afternoon, we stepped on land as soon as possible, and Marian seemed happy as her feet touched African soil. I think for her it was like coming home actually to be in the land where her forefathers had lived for hundreds of years.

In the harbor, as in so many tropical harbors, there were scores of boys busily diving after coins thrown in the water by the passengers. The Dakar boys are very clever, somewhat like the boys in Honolulu. At the pier, we saw nothing especially interesting, but we could see the city a short distance away and started to walk in that direction.

As we approached the city, the native women appeared interested in and curious about Marian, their sister who was smartly dressed in European style. Their curiosity made Marian feel shy, so we hastened our steps and found a little restaurant, where we stopped for a refreshing drink.

Immediately a large number of natives surrounded us, offering many things for sale. Marian wanted to return to our liner, but I urged her to stay and suggested that we take a taxi drive around Dakar. As we drove farther into the city, we could see the real African women, elegantly adorned in shining robes of many colors, with artistic coiffures. Many of them were very stout, but we noticed that they were all proud of their figures and carried their weight with native dignity. The men were marvel-

RECITAL ON BOARD THE "S.S. AUGUSTUS" ON THE TRIP TO SOUTH AMERICA.

ously built, tall and slender, and they went about with sure steps, their bodies swaying in rhythmic movements.

We drove first to the famous market place, where flowers of many colors and rare fruits were invitingly displayed; but the smell of fish was so terrific that we did not linger long. Near by we saw boys playing games with buttons in the sand, and as we stood watching them, one boy turned to us and said in fluent French, *"Oui, monsieur, ça c'est Sénégal."* ("Yes, mister, this is Senegal.")

Taking our car again, we went on, glad to get away from the smelly market place. We drove with no particular destination in mind. Suddenly we could hear the sound of drums in the distance, and we asked our chauffeur to drive us in that direction. As we drew near, we could see a large crowd of people sitting and standing in a sandy place, and the chauffeur told us there was a real tom-tom in progress. We stopped and, standing on the running board, watched this fascinating and unique performance, which, we were told, was not given for tourists but for the natives' own amusement. A small drum orchestra of five or six men was playing strongly rhythmic dance music; and two scantily clothed girls danced in their bare feet. The people were much interested in this performance, and when one of the girls did an especially exotic movement, the natives threw their hats, shawls, and shoes to her as an expression of thanks and admiration.

In this place, we had an opportunity of studying the many different types of people. To Marian the strange and artistically made coiffures began to take on a real elegance, and the bright-colored dresses seemed to be the only kind that suited this environment. The proud gestures of the men seemed to indicate something of a hidden kingliness. It was easy to forget the taxi, the city of Dakar, and to imagine that we were deep in the African jungle, taking part in a strange performance steeped in old African culture.

While we were eating our dinner in a restaurant in the city, I was surprised to feel a touch under our table; it was a little boy who had sneaked into this forbidden place quietly to offer his wares. As I was trying to purchase something from him, the proprietor discovered the boy and threw him out.

The sun began to go down, the darkness suddenly fell, and it was almost time for us to leave for our liner. On the way to the pier, a native boy, standing in a regal attitude, smoking a cigarette, came over to me and said he was hungry. I gave him five lire, and he looked very much pleased. Then he turned to Marian and said exactly the same words, and she also gave him a shiny silver piece. The boy thanked her, smiled, and again turned to me, saying, "Don't you understand, I am hungry . . . more hungry."

So in Dakar also, life goes on—"I am hungry . . . more hungry."

Our liner steamed boldly away from the port of Dakar. The trip from Africa to South America had begun, and soon the soft trade winds were blowing sufficiently to refresh us as we came near the equator. Small flying fishes darted around our steamer as it speeded along. They glittered in the bright sunshine, and for hours Marian and I enjoyed watching them. They seemed to be the only sign of life in this great expanse of water. The sun rose straight up in the early mornings, and in the evenings we saw the wonderful picturesque Southern Cross, which was just visible in the sky. Every day seemed to be about the same, always the brilliant sun, the same warm winds, and occasionally a tropical shower that lasted only a few moments. Every passenger was resting and enjoying life to the full in his own way.

Two days before we arrived at Rio de Janeiro, Marian gave a recital on the ship for the benefit of the seamen. It is especially satisfying to give a recital in the environment of a modern luxury liner.

The last day, after the captain's dinner and much gaiety and festivity, there was a large dance. Since I do not dance, I stood on the deck by myself, studying the star-filled sky. Once, when I happened to look around, I saw four men carrying a coffin; the men walked silently, with bared heads, and soon disappeared inside the ship.

"Who is dead?" I asked myself as I looked to see if anyone was near by. A woman came with quick steps, asking, "Who is dead?" The sorrowful news spread like fire; the dance was stopped, and we all looked at each other, wondering which of our ship companions was in that coffin.

"Oh, you are here. I am so glad," "I am very happy to see *you*," and similar exclamations were soon heard. At last we found out that the dead person was a prominent envoy who took his meals at the captain's table and, at the last dinner, had been feeling very gay. Why did death knock at his cabin door?

The high cone-shaped mountains near Rio could be seen through the mist; the very high natural monument, Corcovado Mountain, on which stands the figure of Christ, especially was visible from a great distance. From where we were, the figure seemed, at first, to be in the form of a cross, but as we got a clearer view, we noticed that the cross was formed by the holy figure's outstretched, welcoming arms.

As we approached the harbor, the great rocks took on fantastic and varied forms, and we saw that, among its high hills and mountains, the city is divided into different parts, each with its own beach. The restless waves brush constantly on the yellow sea sand. The unusual beauty of this gorgeous country seemed to make us forget all about the recitals to come.

Marian and I thoroughly enjoyed a most charming place, the botanical gardens, which were planted and designed personally by one of the Brazilian emperors many years ago. The way they have been planned and planted is wonderful, different from any gardens we had ever seen. One gets a splendid perspective from any of the corners. The main entrance is lined with a broad avenue of royal palms. Twilight was falling while we were there, and when the screeching tropical birds were no longer heard, the frogs sang their evening songs in the near-by pools. The darkness came quickly, and as it deepened a feeling of peace and harmony that no words can possibly express came over us.

Marian enjoyed the Hotel Gloria especially. From her windows she had a view commanding the harbor, one of the loveliest in the world. On the terrace outside the large dining room, we talked and laughed in the shelter of the rustling palms.

We made some unusual trips over roads leading through jungles inhabited by wild animals and big snakes. In many of these jungles, no human being has ever touched foot.

Marian and I left Rio de Janeiro one fine evening for São Paulo. We were sorry we couldn't do the trip in daylight, for we both wanted to see the exciting beauty of the jungle.

At the hotel in Rio, we had often been told to be sure to see the great snake farm when we got to São Paulo. This snake farm is one of the largest in the world, and laboratories there prepare the serum that is used for snakebites.

One lovely sunny day, when we had some free time, we drove out to this farm, which is beautifully situated several miles out of the city. Down in a valley, we saw the cobras and the smaller snakes and on a hill to the left, the chemical laboratories. Near by was a large basin in which the big snakes and giant poisonous frogs are kept.

Many tourists with their guides were walking around the farm. Presently we found ourselves alone. Marian took some photographs. As we stood watching the snakes, we noticed that one of the biggest ones was trying to get to the top of the wall surrounding the basin, but it seemed to be too high for him. We observed the snake's movements closely as he tried again and again. He fell down, got up and wriggled his way to one corner of the basin. We were much surprised to see him suddenly stand straight up. Almost immediately his head was over the wall, and with great force he swung his tail up and was free.

Marian was standing so near that the snake's head could plainly be seen as it lay on top of the wall; she took some steps back, aiming her camera so as to get several views of the fascinating serpent. She did not seem to be in the least afraid but was very tense and, with curiosity, looked the snake straight in the eyes. The snake lay still a few moments, then started slowly winding toward the road, probably intending to get into the great park and the forest on the other side.

We were still the only persons in sight, and I asked Marian to come away quickly, but, as usual, she was very calm and made no effort to leave. I ran down the hill to get the caretaker. I told him of the big snake's escape, but he smiled incredulously, saying that such a thing had never happened before, and he didn't think it was possible. I excitedly told him that it really had happened and urged him to come at once. Catching hold of his sleeve, I pulled him along, and we ran up the hill.

The snake by this time was gliding along the road, wriggling in the sand. The caretaker was astounded. Marian was just a few yards from the snake, still busy taking pictures.

The caretaker ran to the snake and hurriedly grabbed him by the neck. Pointing a scolding finger at him, he said, *"No liberdada."* ("No freedom for you.") The snake twisted himself around the keeper's body, but the man still held him by the neck and finally unwound him, and threw him back in the basin. Marian came closer and, with intense interest, watched the tired snake go at once to the pool and drink water just as a cat does.

The keeper thanked me kindly for telling him of the snake's escape and asked us to come down and see the cobras. Forty boxes of wild cobras, captured in the forests, had just arrived. Forcing open one side of a box, the keeper threw the snakes across the little canal into the basin, which had a small island in the center. On this island we could see the cone-shaped houses that were to be the homes of the reptiles. The cobras at first huddled together in one place, wriggling angrily.

In distributing the snakes to their various homes, the caretaker used a long stick with a hooked end. Standing on the lower level, he first carefully studied the movements of the cobras, looking for a place to jump onto the island where they were. Finally he leaped over the canal. Immediately the snakes began to stick their heads up, their eyes fastened treacherously on their keeper. Quickly, and, it seemed, with no time to spare, he threw each one into his house.

At last only one was left. The keeper cleverly picked him up by the neck with the long hooked stick and walked toward us. We, of course, stood spellbound during this strange performance. Coming near us, the keeper pressed with force on the snake's throat, showing us the wide-open mouth with two large teeth lying against its roof. He took a pincers in his hand and, shoving it in between the roof of the mouth and the poisonous teeth, pressed them forward. This brought the teeth into a certain position so that the poison, in clear crystal drops, began to fall slowly on the sand.

By this time, Marian and I were feeling ill and decided that we had had quite enough of this snake exhibition. We thanked the caretaker for giving us such a dramatic show and drove to a bar, where Marian had her refreshing orange juice and I my cognac.

A year later, I met a friend who had visited the snake farm in São Paulo. He told me that the caretaker still enjoys telling tourists the story of how one of the largest snakes got loose and was captured just when Marian Anderson was visiting there.

Buenos Aires is without doubt one of the liveliest musical cities. The season is short but concentrated

[198]

and of an amazing variety, including opera, orchestral performances, recitals, and countless other attractions. The richness of their musical opportunities has educated the public to be one of the most critical in the world. Musical taste is on a high level, and the audiences are very fastidious. Many famous artists have met with disapproval, among them Caruso, whose first operatic performance was a catastrophe, though later he was very successful there. If one realizes that the Lener string quartet, for instance, plays thirty-six recitals in one season in Buenos Aires, he then has some idea of the importance of good music in the city.

Marian Anderson was quite successful, despite the fact that Lily Pons and other well-known singers were there at the same time. Miss Anderson gave twelve recitals in seven weeks. The last one took place in the city's largest movie theater, the Rex, at eleven o'clock on a Sunday morning. Even I began to think that that was "too much." But it was not. The theater was crowded; every seat was taken. The crowds were so immense that when we left the theater we were in danger, for we had no police protection.

Again at Montevideo, capital of Uruguay, Miss

Anderson was very popular. At the last recital, she was to sing with an orchestra, which was to be conducted by a well-known musician from Buenos Aires. He went to Montevideo two days before the recital date in order to rehearse. It so happened that after the first rehearsal he called our manager, Iriberri, saying that he was not satisfied with the musicians that he had to work with. Marian and I did not pay much attention to this, for it often happens that a conductor is not altogether pleased with an orchestra unfamiliar to him.

We arrived at Montevideo on the morning of the recital. We were to rehearse at noon, but, instead, we found the big orchestra sitting there alone. The conductor could be found nowhere. We waited an hour, and when he did not show up, we began to get restless, thinking perhaps he had met with an accident. On inquiring at the hotel where he stayed, we were told that he did not respond to any calls but that the key was inside the locked door. The day was nearly over, and still there was no conductor; so I thought the best way was to inform the orchestra members that I would play Miss Anderson's accompaniments on the piano.

This was the only wise thing to do. If any of the

purchasers of tickets wanted their money refunded on account of this change, they could have it. Evidently the conductor was right when he thought this orchestra would not be a popular attraction. Only three tickets were returned, and, to our surprise, thirty more tickets were sold!

Later that night, after the recital, Marian and I happened to meet the runaway conductor on the street. He apologized to Miss Anderson for not conducting. It was too late for any arguments, and we all began to laugh—why, I certainly do not know.

One of the most unusual and interesting dance recitals we have ever seen was given by the seventeen-year-old Spanish dancer, Carmen Amaya, in Buenos Aires. Carmen is extremely popular in South America. Every time she gives a performance the house is sold out. She holds an audience intensely under her spell. She appeared in the United States for the first time in 1941.

When it is time to begin a performance, she makes the audience wait. This is done purposely in order to let a silence fall before the people hear the sound of her castanets. At first, this sound is very soft, from off stage; but before she enters, it increases, of course, in a big crescendo. On stage, she stands perfectly still for a moment or two. She is gaily dressed in a colorful costume, with her jet-black hair combed à la Spanish and fastened with many different-colored combs. Her smile is curious and happy. She begins a totally improvised dance and gradually works up to a terrifically wild climax, when, in the middle of the dance, the many combs begin to fly around the stage, her hair becomes disheveled, and her dress is tossed about as though struck by a hurricane. The smiling lips take on a cruel, tigerish expression, and her soft, dark eyes seem to send out gleams of light. When she suddenly stops dancing with a typical Spanish gesture, the people go wild with ecstasy.

Since Marian and I were sitting in a box, it soon became known that the great singer was present. When Carmen danced an extra number, she came close to the footlights and, with a graceful movement of her arm, pointed up to Miss Anderson, announcing in a loud voice that the next dance would be dedicated to the American artist. This was met with a storm of applause, and soon she was

[202]

dancing another number, improvised like the first. It was as though she were floating on waves of music; her movements were wonderfully smooth and flowing. This dance ended with a climax unlike those of the other dances; it was more like the climax in a great chorus of voices.

After the program was finished, Marian and I went backstage, a thing that Marian seldom does. In the little dressing room, we met a girl who, close up, looked very small, much smaller than she appeared on the stage. She was tender and sweet and, having just finished dancing, was trembling from exertion and as excited as a little captured bird. "Look at my fingers," she said to us in a pitiful voice. "They are so very sore after continually playing the castanets. And, besides, I am so foolish that when I hear the sound of a castanet anywhere, I cannot rest until I play with them. I feel forced to do so."

I told her I should like to have an autographed photograph. She gave me a picture but did not autograph it. I said, "Please, Carmen, write your name on it." She quickly answered, "I should really like to, but I am sorry, I cannot write." I thanked her for the picture, and whenever I look at it, I imagine I see a beautiful dedication in good handwriting. I often think that to put a thing down in words is not always necessary if one has enough imagination to read unwritten lines.

AMERICA

NOTHING IN THE WORLD IS SO DIFficult as sustaining a friendship while one is touring constantly. The small, perplexing situations, the restless existence tend to make one nervous and irritable. It isn't easy always to maintain a calm demeanor. I frankly admit that two people of my own temperament, traveling together over an extended period, couldn't keep up a friendly relationship. But I was fortunate in having Marian as a partner. She has an extremely calm nature. Her understanding of human beings and the vibrations of their souls makes it possible for her to overlook many defects in human character. Minor differences that came up between us disappeared like soap bubbles

[207]

bursting in the air, and the following day, neither of us even remembered them.

If you would like to picture Miss Anderson as a traveler, think of a cold, misty morning about 6 A.M. in Chicago. Miss Anderson stands up in the train, looking very sleepy, and is the last one to leave the car. The large collar of her fur coat is turned up, and in her left arm she carries a big bunch of magazines, including *Life, Ladies' Home Journal, The American Home,* several newspapers, and a book or two. In the other hand, she carries her handbag, which is usually so crammed full of things, including opened and unopened letters, that it is impossible to close it.

If one supposes that the bag is much too small and that a larger one could be closed, he is much mistaken. Each time she gets a bigger bag, it is still too small to carry all the articles she wants to put in it, and so it, too, has to be left open. Behind her come the train porters, with fifteen pieces of luggage, and I am sure that no one could possibly guess what they contain. First comes the very large one that is packed with her clothes, then a phonograph, a recording machine, a radio, a sewing machine, and some smaller items, including an electric iron, usually packed in a hatbox, and a few cooking utensils! She once told me that machines seem to take the place of animals that she might otherwise want to take but that would be difficult to carry on long tours.

There is a big difference between the way a tourist travels and the way an artist travels. The tourist is free to go where he desires, but an artist must go where the concert manager directs. The tourist can stay in one place until he feels like moving on; the artist must leave a place according to schedule, no matter how much he may feel like staying.

One of the machines that Miss Anderson perhaps uses most is the sewing machine, for she likes to make pajamas and slacks; any other kind of sewing she seldom attempts. This at least gives Marian something to do in uninteresting hotel rooms.

On trains, Miss Anderson sits quiet and rests as much as possible. Sometimes, when the time seems to drag, we play rummy, and the winner gets the big sum of ten cents. Marian accuses me of winning all the time, but the truth is that she usually has wonderful cards, including the flying deuces, though she doesn't always use them in the right way.

Very often it happens that people come to Marian, asking for her autograph, especially the waiters from the dining car. The waiters are all very proud to have menus signed by her, and she never gets tired of writing her name on them. After a recital, she takes a small table in the artists' room and writes and writes until her nice schoolgirl handwriting vanishes into some kind of unreadable scrawl.

This subject of autographing is one we have often discussed, and she knows that I am not in favor of overdoing this sort of thing. Occasionally I make an effort to interfere, but all the schoolgirls give me such terrible looks that all I can do is stand aside and wait until she is through.

Marian Anderson uses some of her time on trains reading letters. She usually has time to read only the important ones, but once in a while she enjoys a few from admirers or casual correspondents. Some of these are so absurd or pitiful that they make us feel like either laughing or crying.

Many, of course, are letters asking for financial help. The writers make no bones about requesting it in a bold, pointed manner; but some are cleverer than others in their approach. One lady in Denmark wrote as follows: "Please send me twenty thousand dollars, as I intend to open a flower shop in your honor, and I shall call the place 'Marian.' It will be good publicity for you."

Another, from Sweden, was written by someone who called himself Brother John. It said: "I am a reverend in a big church of almost two hundred people. The church is now in bad shape. It needs painting, and a new roof, and lots of other things too. Please come and give a concert. I am sure it will be sold out to the very last ticket, and this will be a great help to us. And I would like to ask one more favor, would you please also give a second concert? My winter overcoat is in an awful condition and needs much fixing."

One of the most amazing letters, about twelve pages long, was from a woman. The writer tried to tell all through the letter just how great a sinner Miss Anderson is and what a wrong life she is leading; but, according to the writer, there was a way for her to learn to walk the right road. If Miss Anderson would come to see the woman, she would open heaven's gates for her.

There are numerous letters of this kind. To read them gives one the opportunity of seeing the funny side of life.

But there are also some serious letters that sound an echo in Miss Anderson's soul. She willingly helps unfortunate people. Many cripples owe her a debt of gratitude for crutches; many of the sick thank her for medical care, and many relief funds, for her interest and her help. All such deeds she does in greatest secrecy. Her checks are never mentioned in the newspapers, and no one ever knows of them except her lawyer, Mr. Hubert Delany. (Mr. Delany is a childhood friend of hers, a fine, artistic gentleman with a bright mind and a deep understanding of life, who, by his many excellent suggestions, helps Marian immensely.) Miss Anderson's generosity and also her desire to remain anonymous were shown, for instance, when she gave a large check to the Finnish war relief. It was done quietly, with the request that it should not be made public.

Many, many people silently send Marian grateful thoughts, blessing her good heart.

MY LITTLE FAMILY" IS A PHRASE Marian often uses. She thinks of her family wherever she goes, and she takes care of her "little family" in a most thoughtful, charming way.

Who are "my little family"? Marian is the eldest of three sisters. Ethel is short and a little large for her height, but she has a most friendly and hearty laugh, of the kind that usually comes natural to stout people. She enjoys working about the kitchen, especially when a party of friends are invited for an evening; then she sits on a small chair beside the sandwiches and other delicious food. Her mind is directed on household affairs, and she bakes the most tasty and attractive-looking cakes. Her husband, Jimmy, likes to point out that Ethel also has a marvelous voice. I am sure that he is prouder of Ethel's voice than of all Marian's artistry. "You ought to hear Ethel sing; that's something!" he says. They have a three-year-old son who is the "cleverest child in the world," and whom everyone, including Aunt Marian, tries to spoil.

Marian's sister Alyce is a different type entirely; she likes lovely dresses and enjoys social life and is interested in politics. Her laughter is contagious. It is she who takes care of Marian's correspondence.

But the central figure in this family is Marian's mother. (Marian's father died when she was a child.) Marian adores and has the greatest admiration for her, admiration such as is seldom seen in this day. The welfare of her mother is first in Marian's mind. She looks after her as she would a little child, and I have heard her say, "Be a nice girl and go to sleep, it is nine o'clock," and other similar words of loving care. I believe that the most difficult thing for Marian is to be separated from her dear mother. She is her last thought of the day, and her first thought in the morning. Letters cannot come too often from her mother, and when they do arrive, Marian seems to have a happier day.

[214]

It is Marian who sees that her mother is dressed in the best furs and most becoming clothes, because she likes to have her make a good appearance.

The first time I met Marian's mother was in Paris. Marian and I were at the depot, waiting at the gate for the train which was to bring her from Le Havre.

"Oh, look, there she is! But I didn't remember her being so small," Marian said.

In her character, Mrs. Anderson has much in common with the reticence, calmness, and unbounded faith of her famous daughter. She doesn't talk very much, but when she does say something, one can readily see that her thoughts are deep and original, are always carefully and smoothly expressed, and leave nothing to be explained. While she was in Paris, I accompanied her on various sightseeing trips.

One night in the hotel, Marian and I were discussing whether she should give three recitals in Paris. Marian said three were too many; but I disagreed. I was sure three recitals would not be "too many," and, in fact, was positive they would be successful. In my endeavor to convince Marian, I raised my voice and got a little excited. Marian's

[215]

mother, who was present, left the room, and waited for two hours in the bathroom while we continued the discussion. Marian at last said yes.

I was very sorry that Mrs. Anderson had to remain in the other room for so long, and when everything was settled and she came out, I said, "I am not bad any more. Please excuse me."

She answered, "Shouldn't Marian do what she wants to do?"

"Surely, but Marian doesn't know Europe; here everyone loves art, and there can never be too much," I retorted.

When the much-discussed recitals were over, Marian warmly thanked me and said that I had been right, even though her mother did have to stay in the bathroom for two hours so as not to hear our discussion.

The next time I met Mrs. Anderson was in her little home in Philadelphia. When we were sitting at the dinner table, she asked the blessing in a soft voice, rather quickly, but it was evident that the old religious ceremony was kept alive by everyday use. She is also the guardian who sees that other customs of her old home are kept in force. For Thanksgiving, there is the traditional turkey; for Christmas, duck; and for Easter, brightly colored eggs.

The third time I had the pleasure of meeting her was to me the most important. Marian had leased a house in the country, and her mother was staying there with her. She was, of course, very happy. Since I happened to be the only other guest, this afforded me the opportunity to become much better acquainted with Mrs. Anderson during the two months that I was there, coaching Marian in new songs. Generally I found Mrs. Anderson reading large, thick books of at least six hundred pages, which she told me she found most wonderful reading. She is a woman of considerable education and was a schoolteacher, in her youth, in Virginia.

She often sat out on the veranda, and, although reading, she watched quite closely what was going on around her. She is interested in everything. "Do you see the smoke over there, Kosti? I was just wondering if that train is going to or from Danbury." "Do you think, Kosti, that the crooked tree near the fence is an apple tree or that those yellow things are leaves?" She was not satisfied until I went over and looked and brought back a yellow apple.

[217]

Once, when the servants had a day off, for diversion Marian was going to be cook. I suggested that we eat in the big kitchen, but the dining-room table had already been nicely laid. Marian was therefore obliged to go back and forth to the kitchen, and her mother would ask such questions as, "What is she doing now?" and, "Can I come out and help you, Marian?" She would get up and go into the kitchen to help, and I also went. So we three were there together, while our food on the table was getting cold.

One night there came a telephone call that two of Marian's horses had broken loose and were on the road untended. Marian and I went at once to try to get them and bring them back where they belonged. Mrs. Anderson wanted to go with us; she was afraid there might be some danger. This Marian strongly objected to and requested her mother to stay in the house and watch from the windows, which she did.

Soon after this, I composed a piano number called "A Friend." I also composed a series of three pieces inspired by life in a pool. The first I called "Water Lily," the second, "The Goldfishes' Burial." "But what shall I call the third one?" I asked them. They both gave several suggestions, and finally Mrs. Anderson said she thought it sounded like a real frog frolic: so I called it "Frog Frolic" and thanked her for the excellent suggestion.

Who are Marian Anderson's friends? That is a difficult question to answer. Like other great artists, she has many friends who ask for tickets before a recital, and, of course, she has many friends who pay her flattering compliments afterward. There are even some who say, "I am Marian Anderson's friend," but whom Marian doesn't know at all.

Marian's heart is like a little golden casket that is extremely difficult to open; perhaps no one will ever do that. But everyone who knows her well has a sure feeling that in this sacred place is a most valued and exquisite pearl. She guards it carefully in order, one feels, that no living being can come near enough to disturb the great calmness of her soul.

A good friend of Marian's since her childhood is Harry Burleigh, the well-known singer and composer. When Marian returns from a long voyage, he is always at the pier to give his friendly greeting. We generally hear the words "Hello, Marian!

Hello, Kosti! It is nice to see you again." And when he is sure Marian is all right, he departs; and we seldom see him again for some time. His is a soul whose presence and good will we both feel very near to us.

Marian and I were invited to the White House twice. The circumstances were quite different in each case. The first time, Marian Anderson sang at a small dinner party given in the President's private apartments. The second time was when King George and Queen Elizabeth visited at the White House in 1939.

On the first occasion, the house was quite still. We were downstairs, waiting to be called up to the President's private salon on the second floor. We walked around the official reception rooms, looking at every detail. There was a dignified atmosphere of tradition and also of the democratic spirit. The President's wife had courteously invited Miss Anderson's mother to this intimate recital. The look of happiness and the anticipation in Mrs. Anderson's face are difficult to describe.

At first, Marian and I were ushered into the music room. There was a large, comfortable sofa at one

MISS ANDERSON AS SHE APPEARS DURING HER AMERICAN TOURS.

side of the fireplace, on which the President was sitting and enjoying the great fire. His sure and strong handshake gives one a feeling of confidence, and his friendly, warm glance is good for the heart. That we were in the presence of a big personality no one could doubt.

On this occasion, Marian sang with a special fire and power. I have often noticed that when a well-known person, or one whom she especially honors, is before her, she sings with exceptional brilliance and fullness. By this I do not mean that Miss Anderson does not always give her best, no matter how small the audience may be; but there seems to be a special inspiration for her in the presence of big personalities.

After she sang, there was a very touching scene. Mrs. Roosevelt, our charming hostess, took Marian's mother by the hand, and led her over and introduced her to the President. I shall never forget seeing these two ladies enter the room. Mrs. Roosevelt's manner was sure and free, as becomes a woman of the world, happy to welcome the mother of America's best-known singer. In all of Mrs. Anderson's being, there was evident the feeling that this was one of the greatest moments in her life.

Her face reflected her gratitude and the pride she felt.

I had the opportunity of speaking with the President for a few moments, during which he asked my nationality and said some kind words about the Finnish people. This was before the Finnish war, when the chief thing all Americans honored Finland for was that she was the only country that paid her debts.

The other time we visited the White House was much more formal. The whole place was busy and crowded. This time Miss Anderson and I were ushered into the President's private room on the first floor. Later we were brought to a room where the other artists had gathered, awaiting their turns to perform. Lawrence Tibbett, of the Metropolitan Opera, was one of the leading artists; another was Alan Lomax, the cowboy singer, who walked nervously around with his instrument hung about his neck. His coat was wrinkled by the cord, and when I straightened it for him, he gave me a smile and continued nervously to walk. Kate Smith, of the radio, also sang.

The artists had not been told just where the king and queen would be sitting so that we could give a special bow in honor of them; and the occasion was so very brilliant and there were so many dazzling decorations that when Miss Anderson and I got upon the stage, it was quite impossible to see exactly where the honored guests were. I whispered to Marian, "Where is the king?" and hoped that her sharp eyes would catch a glimpse of him; but receiving no answer, I made a bow in the same direction that she did.

Schubert's "Ave Maria" made a lasting impression and, of course, received enormous applause. After the program, every artist was presented to Their Royal Majesties. The queen resembled a real fairy-tale princess, dressed in a magnificent chiffon gown embroidered with shimmering white sequins; and her diadem and jewels outshone all the rest. Her almost childlike smile, so appealing and now so familiar to all Americans, was much in evidence when she warmly greeted Miss Anderson. The king looked slender and amazingly young.

Marian made a deep curtsy, with which she afterward admitted she herself was not well satisfied. She remarked on her way home that what one does well at home one not always does so very well before a king and queen. I was surprised when she told me that for some time she had been practicing the curtsy.

The program had been very well arranged and was most enthusiastically received. It went to prove what a marvelous organizer Mrs. Roosevelt really is. She is not only a very prominent and important factor in the social and political life of the United States but also an ideal hostess. The many difficult and complicated situations with which she is often confronted are met with an unusual frankness and a thoughtfulness that enable her to untie the most complex knots with great facility.

As a graceful token of thanks, President and Mrs. Roosevelt sent Marian and me beautifully framed autographed photographs of themselves, a gesture that we both deeply appreciated.

To A PERSON BORN IN FINLAND, AS I was, the race question is difficult to understand. In my country, there are no colored people, and the number of Jews is small. But race prejudice in this day has grown to the extent that leaders in cultural and religious life all over the world are increasingly alarmed about it. The two countries in which I have been where the race question is most prevalent are the United States and Germany.

As a non-Aryan, Marian Anderson did not sing in Germany after the new regime came into power. She had been invited to do so in Berlin with the Berlin Philharmonic, but since she did not wish to be involved in any trouble that might come up, the invitation was not accepted.

Before coming to this country in 1935, I was faced with a perplexing problem having to do with race. Before going to Europe, Marian Anderson had had a Negro accompanist. The friction that might be caused by the appearance of a white and a Negro person on the concert stage together in America was a difficulty. Finally, our manager wrote Marian that a recital with a white accompanist was quite impossible.

This was the first time that Marian explained to me that we might meet with some dissatisfaction in appearing on a stage together.

"But can't we at least try to change this prejudice? I am ready to do my part," I told her.

"It is too deeply rooted. Two people cannot solve it alone; it would take much time. But we can perhaps help bring it about," Marian answered.

"But for you, art comes first, and then the other question; isn't that true?" I asked Marian.

She answered this by going to her desk, sitting down, and writing this wire to her manager in New York: "Mr. Vehanen and I arrive in New York on December 17."

It was a clear answer to my question. Knowing that, after several hundred concerts together, we had developed an understanding of programs and their projection, Marian resolved to use me.

We embarked on the beautiful *Ile de France*. At first, as was the usual custom, we went to the head waiter to make our reservations in the dining room. There happened to be an English-speaking family doing the same thing, and I heard the woman say with a pitying voice, "Look, there is Europe's famous Marian Anderson. Poor girl, I wonder where she will eat."

I was not the only one who heard this remark. The head waiter also heard it, and he answered loudly, in an irritated voice, "A place in the large dining room is reserved for Miss Anderson, but," as he looked at the woman, "there are others in the smaller ones that you can have if you wish."

Marian and I enjoyed our meals in the elegant main dining room, and everyone was friendly.

In the afternoon, the sea was rough, and the big liner began to rock from side to side. We had just had our tea and were on the way to our cabins. In going down a stairway, Marian's heel slipped on the stair, and she fell down five or six steps. I tried my best to catch her, but it happened too quickly.

She was lying on the floor, helpless, with a fractured foot.

This with our first American recital scheduled in two weeks!

Since Marian couldn't walk, she was obliged to stay in her cabin. But she had been asked to sing at a benefit concert on the ship, and she did not want to break her promise; so she was placed in an invalid's chair and taken to the stage. Here she stood up on one foot, let her magnificent voice fill the large hall, and made a great success.

On our arrival in New York, she tried to walk in some way, but the pain was too terrific. We wondered how she could give the scheduled recitals. But she never seriously considered canceling them. With her broad smile, she said, "I shall sing."

Special arrangements were made for her Town Hall appearance December 30. The curtain was lowered before the recital began so that she might be brought upon the stage in the chair. As she sat in the artists' room in the invalid chair, she was calm and acted as though nothing had happened. Just what the waiting audience was thinking no one knew. When the time came to begin, the nurse

[230]

and I helped her to the side of the piano, where she stood up bravely on one foot, with her arm resting on the piano. In this position she sang the full program. When the recital was half over, she explained to the audience why it was necessary to use the curtain. She apologized for her stiff bows and for leaning on the piano. But it marked the beginning of Marian Anderson's sensational success in the United States.

Although we both came to this country directly from the Hotel Majestic in Paris, not one hotel in New York at first opened its doors to Miss Anderson; so she was obliged to live in Harlem. She didn't seem to mind and never uttered a word of complaint. As Miss Anderson traveled through the United States, however, she met with the same difficult hotel question. This naturally caused her considerable embarrassment and discomfort.

It did not take very long before one of her anonymous friends arranged to have an apartment reserved for her in one of the older and better-known New York hotels. Soon the hotel accepted her as a regular guest. This action helped to give the hotel the high cultural reputation that it so well deserves. I am pleased to relate that many other hotels throughout the country soon followed this example and made her welcome.

A few went only halfway. When we arrived at certain hotels where rooms had been reserved for us, the manager would whisper in my ear, "Please . . . ! We hope that you will take your meals in your rooms." We accepted the situation as gracefully as we could.

But one time I really was angry. We were in Duluth and had a couple of hours to wait before train time. We were hungry, and there was a hotel near the depot. We went in and walked toward the dining room, but the little snub-nosed waiter at the door told us that the dining room was closed. I could see people inside eating, but the waiter stubbornly insisted that the dining room was not open. Miss Anderson stood calmly a little to one side, smiling, and no doubt thinking how small the soul of such a man must be. I asked the waiter, "Do you know what you are doing?" He only shrugged his shoulders. "Where is the hotel manager and the telephone?" I asked.

I called the manager and told him how Miss Anderson was being treated in his hotel, so that not even food was obtainable. After my explanation, the manager came and called down the waiter and gladly showed us into the dining room. While we were there, the stubborn waiter came in three different times and apologized to Miss Anderson. Without saying an unkind word, she merely looked at him and said, "You didn't know any better."

Once I was invited to dinner at a prominent person's home in Washington, D. C. It was just before the English king and queen were guests at the White House. Opposite me sat a woman wearing large diamond bracelets. After she learned who I was, she said to me with an ironic smile, "Aren't you ashamed to travel around with a colored woman? Don't you know that soon no one will give you invitations or want to be in your presence?"

"Don't you understand," I answered, "that your despicable, narrow thinking makes it impossible for you even to enter the doors through which Miss Anderson enters?"

She blushed and was terribly irritated. "You cannot name one place where the doors are open to Miss Anderson and not to me," she said haughtily.

"Oh, yes, I can. The doors of the White House are open to welcome her when Queen Elizabeth and

King George of Great Britain will be there," I quickly answered, "and they are closed to you, I am sure."

At this reply, she slammed her hands on the table, rattling her bracelets, and exclaimed in a furious voice, "That's really too much!"

Our host gave me a smile and a wink on the sly. I turned to speak to another dinner guest.

Another time I was invited to a doctor's home. Through some misunderstanding, I thought Miss Anderson had also been invited, and I was waiting for her to arrive. Finally I asked the hostess where Miss Anderson could be. She answered me in a short, curt manner, saying, "Miss Anderson is not invited. She can never come to this house."

I was most astonished and naïvely asked the reason why.

"But, Mr. Vehanen, we are aristocrats," she boldly said.

"What do you mean by aristocrats?" I questioned.

"My family has been in this country a hundred and seventy-five years," she proudly answered.

"And is that what you mean by aristocrats?" I asked. "My family has owned the same land in Finland, from father to son, for five hundred years, and still I am not an aristocrat."

I could no longer stay there, for I felt nothing in common with those "aristocratic" people, and I took my hat and left.

From all these little incidents that happened to me during five concert seasons, in which we appeared in more than 150 cities, I felt that I understood the complicated race question less and less; and I have still to understand why the worth of a person seems to depend on the color of the skin. I cannot believe that the heart beats differently in the colored person's breast than it does in the white man's. And I cannot believe that the soul in one is more valuable in the eyes of God, who created all souls equal. But one thing I learned from Miss Anderson's reaction to all this was that a person with her magnificent calmness and her deep understanding and fine character can through her great art help to wipe away many differences of opinion among the various races.

Here Miss Anderson has a powerful weapon—her singing, which uplifts the spirit.

Not only the Negro race but every race ought to be very grateful that a human being such as Miss

Anderson is giving her message of peace to a world filled with hatred and misunderstanding. And the one who is bringing this brotherly message through the universal appeal of music is predestined to go to the very heights.

ONE DAY THE NEWSPAPERS CARRIED the astonishing news that the Daughters of the American Revolution's headquarters in Washington objected to Marian Anderson's giving a recital in their Constitution Hall. This news seemed all the more strange to us, for we knew that Roland Hayes and also some colored dancers had appeared in the very same hall.

Why was this terrible insult put upon Marian Anderson? As we read the papers, we were sitting comfortably in her compartment on the train. A wonderful panorama of the great California mountains and forests was passing before our sight. Miss Anderson laid the paper down, kept looking out the window, and we both remained silent for some time. No one can tell the thoughts that were in her mind at that moment, I think not even herself. She did not discuss this serious question confronting her. There were too many good and beautiful things to talk about.

But the peace that Marian felt was soon disturbed by numerous newspaper reporters and many other people who constantly fired embarrassing questions at Miss Anderson, such as, "How do you feel?" "Do you feel insulted by this refusal?" "What is your attitude toward all this?" and "What do you intend to do?"

Miss Anderson's answer was, "I don't know anything except what you have all seen in the newspapers. I have no opinion to offer."

Then came the great announcement that Mrs. Eleanor Roosevelt had resigned from the D.A.R. A joyful look came into Marian's eyes, and she said to me, "What a wonderful woman she is! She not only knows what is right, but she also does the right thing."

The curious, bold questions these people kept asking Marian were never answered by her, and she still preserved the same attitude.

(*Press Association*)

THE OUTDOOR RECITAL AT THE LINCOLN MEMORIAL, WASHINGTON, EASTER, 1939.

MARIAN ANDERSON AND HER MOTHER BEFORE THE STATUE OF
LINCOLN IN THE LINCOLN MEMORIAL.

A proposal then came from Washington that Miss Anderson should give an outdoor recital there. It so happened at this time that I was taken sick and was brought to a hospital in Washington.

There were many different opinions among Marian's friends about her giving a recital in the open. Some thought, why should she sing outdoors? It would be better not to sing at all. Others thought that it was a marvelous idea and that she should do it.

Miss Anderson telephoned me at the hospital every day from wherever she happened to be, and I knew that she was more against the idea than she was for it. She did not like the thought of doing anything sensational just because of the insult thrust upon her. Four days before the date announced for her appearance at the great Lincoln Memorial, which was to take place on Easter Sunday, 1939, she was still undecided and came very near canceling the arrangements. I have always thought that this was one of her most beautiful characteristics— she is so far removed from anything that might be considered sensational or in opposition to anyone or any organization that for her to oppose the idea of this extraordinary occasion was quite natural. She likes to win any victory purely with the implement of her great art and not mix in anything that may oppose this holy gift.

She traveled to Washington just to see me during a few hours that she had free. Of course, the action of the D.A.R. had been given prominence in the papers, and when she arrived at the station there was a great crowd of people who were, no doubt, in sympathy with her. A police escort led her to the hospital. When she came to my room, we talked this important matter over and decided that it was too late to cancel the recital and step out. "But I do hope that you will be able to accompany me, Kosti," Marian said.

When the big day came, we were escorted to the Lincoln Memorial by several motorcycle police. Here we waited in an inner room. There were several people around us, including Marian's family, and a great feeling of anticipation was in the air. Marian was calm. She stood quiet and held her head high. I went to the piano first to fasten the music, for a soft wind was blowing. When I saw the immense crowd of seventy-five thousand people, then looked at the Steinway piano, I had a feeling that it would be of little use to begin to play, for I was sure that no one could possibly hear it. I also felt how really small a person seems when facing such a gathering, which stretched so far that I could scarcely see the end.

Those with special invitations were admitted to a platform that had been built for the occasion. Many prominent people were there, including Secretary Ickes, Supreme Court Justice Black, Secretary of the Treasury Morgenthau, and several members of Congress. The loud-speakers seemed to stretch their necks out, eager to heighten the sounds. All the important radio stations were represented, and the microphones stood like an army of soldiers guarding the elevated platform where Marian was to stand. Some yards in front of this was a special platform to accommodate the many film operators. The apparatus seemed to be looking with curious, anxious eyes at the place where she would be. Near by were countless photographers, with their cameras pointed in the same direction.

Secretary Ickes came forward and made a speech, in which he said: "There are those even in this great capital of our democratic republic who are either too timid or too indifferent to lift up the light that Jefferson and Lincoln carried aloft. Genius, like justice, is blind. For genius has touched with the tip of her wing this woman, who, if it had not been for the great mind of Jefferson, if it had not been for the great heart of Lincoln, would not be able to stand among us today a free individual in a free land. Genius draws no color line. She has endowed Marian Anderson with such a voice as lifts any individual above his fellows, as is a matter of exultant pride to any race. And so it is fitting that Marian Anderson should raise her voice in tribute to the noble Lincoln, whom mankind will ever honor."

Then Miss Anderson appeared within the central enclosure of the monument. She looked regal and dignified as she came forward with slow steps. She wore a long black velvet dress, her mink coat around her shoulders. When she came to the place where the steps began to descend, she stopped for a moment as she gazed over the enormous gathering of people. Her breath seemed to leave her for that fleeting moment; but I think that those persons who were privileged to see her at that time were much more moved than she was.

She looked slender and beautiful when she emerged between the high marble columns, directly in front of the great Lincoln Memorial, which was

[244]

filled with shadow in the late afternoon light. The statue of Lincoln appeared to be alive on this occasion, and he seemed to be in deep thought, this great man with an exceptionally broad mind. Perhaps the most fitting and appropriate statement he would have made would have been to tell the assembled people that the appearance of Marian Anderson before this countless number of admirers was one of the greatest results of his efforts to make all people free and equal.

Miss Anderson was so deeply moved by the whole scene that she felt that it was not only a recital but something of much greater importance and value, which had a depth of meaning to all mankind. It was a message of peace, a message of understanding that she was destined to bring to a sinful world.

No one who saw her walking that day down the marble steps will ever forget this unusual and wonderful sight; and few can recall it without tears springing to their eyes.

She now stood ready. The first sounds of the piano were powerfully transmitted through the many loud-speakers, sounding as though ten organs were playing. Then she began to sing.

[245]

If human beings in their narrow wisdom closed the door of their small halls, then God in His great wisdom opened the door to His most beautiful cathedral, which was decorated that day as for a festival, with lovely green grass, cherry trees in blossom, the large pool mirroring the blue sky, and light clouds leisurely floating by, a soft wind caressing everyone, colored and white—every human being, rich and poor, the strong and the weak, the good and the bad sharing in the beauties so freely bestowed upon them that glorious Easter Sunday.

A GLOOMY DAWN LOOKED IN through my window. I put my light out; all around me on the floor were pencil shavings, crumpled papers, and on my desk was a stack of written manuscript.

The beauties of nature that, last evening, had been so enchanting were mysteriously covered with soft white fog. Many peaches had fallen during the night, forming a colorful pattern on the grass.

I put the written sheets carefully together, silently opened the door which led to the ground floor, and went out into the yard. There was a lonely path leading up the hill. This is the way I chose to go. The lovely red leaves now were weeping large misty pearls. My shoes got wet, but I paid no attention to that; a yellow falling leaf touched my cheek, but I scarcely felt it; my mind was filled with memories.

Perhaps many important things have been forgotten; perhaps many unimportant things remembered. But I hope the picture of Marian Anderson will be seen clearly enough through my mosaic pattern of our ten years together. The wants of readers are very different; but if one is true, one must follow his own path, and choose his own way in trying to explain happenings that to other people would be seen with quite different eyes.

And when the curtain falls after this colorful time, I feel thankful and rich, rich through many experiences and thankful, most of all, to Marian Anderson.

APPENDIX

IMPORTANT DATES IN MARIAN ANDERSON'S CAREER

1924	Philadelphia Choral Society, Philadelphia
August 26, 1925	Lewisohn Stadium, New York
1925-1926	Town Hall recital; programs with Roland Hayes
1928-1929	Solo groups with Negro chorus in Carnegie Hall, New York; recital in Carnegie Hall
October, 1930	Berlin debut
1930-1931	Recital in Carnegie Hall, New York; series with Hall Johnson Choir; Scandinavian tour
1931-1932	Many concerts in leading cities

	and provincial towns of Scandinavia
1932-September, 1933	American appearances; soloist with Hall Johnson Choir
September, 1933-April, 1934	142 concerts in Denmark, Norway, Sweden, and Finland alone
May, 1934	Paris and London debuts
Summer, 1934	Belgium and Holland
1934-1935	Tour of Poland, Russia, Latvia, Switzerland, Belgium, Austria, Hungary, Italy, and Spain; first Salzburg appearances
December, 1935-March, 1936	Recitals in Town Hall and Carnegie Hall, New York; coast-to-coast American tour
1936	Concerts in London, Paris, Holland, Belgium, and Russia
June, 1936	Concert in Vienna with Bruno Walter; two concerts in Salzburg that summer
1936-1937	Tour of Europe, including Vienna, Budapest, The Hague, and other cities

TWO OF MARIAN ANDERSON'S PROGRAMS

I

Piangero mia sorte ria (Aria from "Julius
Caesar") ....Handel
Siciliana ....Handel
Sento la gioja (Aria from "Armadiji")....Handel

II

Auf der Donau (On the Danube).......Schubert
Die Rose (The Rose)................Schubert
Meeresstille (Calm at sea)............Schubert
Die Männer sind méchant (Men are all the
same) ....Schubert
In der Ferne (Afar)................Schubert

III

Recitative and Aria from "Carmen".........Bizet

Intermission

IV

Cantilena ....Vehanen

Pastorale ....Vehanen

Amuri, Amuri ....Sodero

Vocalise ....Ravel

V

Negro Spirituals:

City Called Heaven......Arranged by Hall Johnson

O Peter, go ring dem bells..Arranged by Burleigh

Sometimes I feel like a motherless child

Arranged by Brown

Honor, Honor.........Arranged by Hall Johnson

Kosti Vehanen at the piano.

* * * * * * *

I

Schubert   Dem Unendlichen

Schubert   Die Vögel

Schubert   Vom Mitleiden Maria

Schubert   Verklärung

II

Wolf	Nun lass uns Frieden
Wolf	Fussreise
Wolf	Wer sein holdes Lieb' verloren
Wolf	Gesang Weylas

III

| Handel | Lucretia |

Intermission

IV

Sibelius	But my bird
Sibelius	Idle Wishes
Sibelius	Solitude
Sibelius	War es ein Traum

V

Negro Spirituals

Arranged by

Johnson	Done foun' my las' sheep
Brown	Dere's no hidin' place down dere
Boatner	Trampin'
Burleigh	Wide River

Kosti Vehanen at the piano.

Review of Miss Anderson's appearance with the New York Philharmonic Orchestra at Lewisohn Stadium, New York City, August 26, 1925. By Francis D. Perkins, New York Herald Tribune, *August 27, 1925.*

A REMARKABLE VOICE WAS HEARD last night at the Lewisohn Stadium. Its possessor was Marian Anderson, a young Negro contralto, who was the only singer chosen from about 300 contestants in the auditions held last June. She appeared as soloist last night before what was estimated as the third largest Stadium audience of the summer. About 7,500 with a good-sized Negro contingent were included in this band of enthusiasts.

Miss Anderson sang "O mio Fernando" from Donizetti's "La Favorita," with the Philharmonic Orchestra, under Willem van Hoogstraten's direction, and a group of spirituals with another Negro

[259]

artist, William King, at the piano. He also accompanied her in three encores.

Miss Anderson is from Philadelphia and a pupil of Giuseppe Boghetti. Last night's was not her first appearance here. She had given a recital at Town Hall on April 23, 1924, but that had hinted little at the astonishing vocal powers displayed by the young singer last night. The present reviewer on that occasion had animadverted on a powerful voice of true contralto quality, in need of some further development, but it had hardly seemed then the voice in a thousand—or shall we say ten thousand or a hundred thousand?—that it appeared to be last night.

A notable feature in Miss Anderson's singing was its entire naturalness; all that she had to do, apparently, was to sing, without any need of apparent effort to fill the Stadium spaces. In high and low notes, there was a full rich quality that carried far; the singer had no more trouble, it seemed, in singing at the Stadium than in singing at Aeolian Hall, but seemed more at her ease, in smoother voice than in the Aeolian Hall audition.

A storm of applause followed the Donizetti number, very meritoriously sung, and Miss Anderson offered Terry's "The Answer" as an encore. But expressively, she seemed most at home in the three spirituals scheduled for her second appearance: Harry T. Burleigh's "Deep River" and "Heav'n" and J. Rosamond Johnson's "Song of the Heart," in a performance characterized by what might be called expressive simplicity. As encores, songs by Liza Lehmann and R. Huntington Woodman followed.

And while Miss Anderson's singing was remarkable as it was, and showed marked progress over the 1924 recital and even over the June auditions, she has still room for further progress. There seemed a slight hint of roughness in some of her lower notes; a certain pitch in her upper register where there was a little tremolo; one place marked by the harsher timbre which has mostly been banished from her voice, while there also seems room for development in interpretation. But after some further study, Miss Anderson should merit a prominent place among singers in active service; she can make a striking impression now, but should not take the plunge into intensive concert work too soon.

Review of Miss Anderson's recital at Carnegie Hall, Sunday afternoon, March 2, 1930. New York Times, March 3.

Marian Anderson, a Negro soprano of natural vocal gifts far beyond the usual endowment of mortals, appeared at Carnegie Hall yesterday afternoon before an audience that scantily filled the large auditorium. How gloriously her tones could fill it these hearers soon testified. Her program was of well-chosen lyrics from Italian, German, French and American composers and a final group of Negro spirituals. William King was the accompanist.

The singer, a native of Philadelphia, first became known there for these spirituals of her race, which she gives with wide range of voice—though she chooses to be known as a contralto—and with rare

[263]

sympathy. Coached by Giuseppe Boghetti in the Italian masters, she became equally versatile in varied classics. From 300 contestants she was chosen in 1925 to sing with the New York Philharmonic at the Stadium.

Two years after her last local recital she returned yesterday between tours South and West. From the first note of the matinee she showed a modest avoidance of the sensational and an artist's refinement of style and taste. In Mozart's "Alleluia" alone was the superb, unforced upper tone lacking the last word in agility. A true mezzo-soprano, she compassed both ranges with full power, expressive feeling, dynamic contrast, and utmost delicacy.

There will be more to say of Marian Anderson should circumstances lead her to European halls for appraisal of natural gifts and cultivation, as in the case of Paul Robeson or Roland Hayes. Yesterday's list, which included songs by Louis Saar and the late Charles Griffes, closed with such folksong arrangements as Burleigh's "O Peter," Johnson's "Little David," Boatner's "Tramping," and Dawson's "Truth about a Child."

Herbert F. Peyser's articles on musical events in Europe, printed in the New York Times, *frequently mentioned Miss Anderson. His account of one of her triumphs follows. This was published, it should be noted, March 10, 1935, some months before her return to New York in December.*

Bᴜᴛ ᴀ ꜱᴇɴꜱᴀᴛɪᴏɴ ᴏꜰ ᴛʜᴇ ᴠɪᴇɴɴᴀ music season, and to date perhaps its most dramatic event, has been the debut here of the colored contralto from Philadelphia, Marian Anderson. In less than two weeks she has given two recitals. The first was attended by a handful. The second was mobbed. It took only one number (the death song from Purcell's "Dido and Aeneas") to effect such a conquest as has not been witnessed here in six months of Sundays. The press has been rhapsodic. "Verbluffend" . . . "stunning" . . . and "phenomenal" are the weakest adjectives in currency. "A black Lilli Lehmann," exclaimed one authority. From the treasury of majestic memories the names of Alice Barbi (Brahms's favorite Liedersinger), Julia Culp and others less resplendent have been freely evoked for something like adequate comparisons. And amazement has grown greater still by the fact that the classics of song literature and even the lyrics of Gustav Mahler form her province.

There can be no question that Miss Anderson, alike by virtue of her great, gorgeous voice, her art of song, the emotional, indeed the spiritual and mystical elements of her nature that repeatedly lend her work the character of a consecration, her dignity, sympathy, and ineffable sincerity of approach, ranks today among the few imposing vocal confrontations of the age. It is by no means impossible to pick flaws in her work, to cavil at this trifle or that. To do so. however, is a good deal like criticizing the pyramids of Egypt because here and there is a stone crumbled or misshapen.

Review of Miss Anderson's first appearance in America after her return from Europe in 1935 (Town Hall, December 30). New York Times, December 31, 1935. Signed "H. T." (Howard Taubman).

LET IT BE SAID AT THE OUTSET: MARian Anderson has returned to her native land one of the great singers of our time. The Negro contralto who has been abroad for four years established herself in her concert at the Town Hall last night as the possessor of an excelling voice and art. Her singing enchanted an audience that included singers. There was no doubt of it, she was mistress of all she surveyed.

The simple facts are better than superlatives, for superlatives are easily abused. Fact one, then, should be the sheer magnificence of the voice itself considered as a musical instrument. It is a contralto of stunning range and volume, managed with suppleness and grace. It is a voice that lends itself to the entire emotional gamut, responsive to delicate nuance and able to swell out with opulence and sonority.

Fact two should be Miss Anderson's musicianship. In a program that encompassed a full group by Handel, another by Schubert, a Verdi aria, a Finnish section and a concluding group of Negro spirituals, she revealed a penetrating command of style. She understood not only the difference in approach between the songs of Handel and Schubert and Sibelius, but the divergences of intent in music by the same composer. Each song was treated as an artistic unit, set forth with care, style and intelligence.

But without deep feeling these other assets would not achieve the grandeur of interpretation that was Miss Anderson's last night, and that should be item three. For Miss Anderson has the transcending quality of all authentic art—a genuine emotional identification with the core of the music. Schubert's "Der Tod und das Maedchen" and "Allmacht" were ennobling in their grandeur. And how many singers have communicated the transfiguring rapture of John Payne's "Crucifixion" as Miss Anderson did last night? It was music-making that probed too deep for words.

To all these things must be added the native good taste of the artist and the simplicity of her personality. Here was a woman of poise and sensibility. The fact that one foot, injured in an accident on board ship on the voyage home, was encased in a cast was never permitted to intrude on the listener's consciousness. She sang with a consciousness of her ability and with a relish of her task that were positively infectious.

It was possible for those of pedantic minds to find minor matters to quibble over, such as the occasional edge in top tones or imperfection of enunciation in foreign languages. They need not be labored here. In the presence of a rich art, pedantry might well be spared.

Limitations of space forbid a detailed discussion of each song on Miss Anderson's program, where columns could be devoted to it with profit. A hint of felicities of phrase and style culled without sequence must be added, however: the sweep of Handel's "Ah spietato," the delicacy of Schubert's "Liebestotschaft," the purity of the contralto's amazing low tones in "Tod und das Maedchen," the coloratura work in Sibelius's "Die Libelle" that remained always in the frame of the song, the laughing quality and exquisite tone coloring in the little Finnish folksong that was an encore after the Suomi group.

Miss Anderson will undoubtedly give many more concerts this season, and there will be opportunity for extended comment on her resources. The reticent accompaniments of Kosti Vehanen must not be overlooked.